HOPE *for* Today,
PROMISES *for* Tomorrow

HOPE *for* Today,
PROMISES *for* Tomorrow

Finding Light Beyond the
Shadow of Miscarriage
or Infant Loss

Teske Drake

Kregel
Publications

For Justin, the father of our five precious children—
three in God's dwelling place, two in our own.
You are the best daddy I know, and it is a miracle
to share this life with you. I love you.

⌇

Contents

Foreword, by Holley Gerth — 11

Introduction: No Broken Promises — 13

1. The Ultimate Promise — 19

2. The Promise of His Love — 27

3. The Promise of His Goodness — 39

4. The Promise of His Purpose — 53

5. The Promise of Comfort — 65

6. The Promise of Peace — 75

7. The Promise of Refinement — 85

8. The Promise of Restoration — 97

9. The Promise of Hope — 107

10. The Promise of Eternity — 115

Appendix A: Becoming a Mommy with Hope — 125

Appendix B: Fellow Mommies' "Hope Stories" — 127

Appendix C: About Mommies with Hope — 137

Acknowledgments — 139

About the Author — 141

Foreword

When a little one slips home to heaven too soon, our hearts ache. I know this pain firsthand and Teske Drake does as well. Perhaps one of the most difficult aspects of this kind of loss is the feeling that we are alone in our hurt. Let me assure you, dear sister, that you are not. More than anything else, this is the gift the following pages offer.

As an author, friend, and fellow griever, Teske will take you by the hand and whisper to your heart what you most need to hear. She will also remind you that even in the darkest moments, God has not forsaken you and He offers hope and healing when it seems impossible.

It has been several years now since we lost our only pregnancy to miscarriage. I would never have chosen this path. But looking back now, I wouldn't trade it. Those are words I never thought I would be able to say. I've come to understand that's what real hope means—that the impossible can come true in our lives.

As a writer, counselor, and life coach, I've seen the same happen for many other women. In the darkest circumstances, the deepest sorrow, we somehow find a resilience and strength we didn't know we had. And we discover we serve a God who is a Redeemer, who lets nothing go to waste, especially when it comes to the hurts in our lives.

I ask one thing of you in this moment: *please keep your heart open*. If you're feeling as I did, then right now you probably want to slam the door of your heart shut, lock it, and throw away the key. Yet it's only by letting love in and allowing gentle truth to find its way to the places inside you that need it most that you'll begin to heal.

Even if you can't open the door to anyone else right now, please let Teske in through the words she's written for you. She's a woman who knows where you are and who longs to walk with you through the next chapters of your journey.

No matter what you've been through, this remains true: you are loved, you have a purpose, you are not alone. I wish Teske and I could both sit down and have a cup of coffee or tea with you today. Until then, know that we're sending our love and prayers to you as fellow travelers on this journey. This isn't what I would have chosen for us to have in common, this hurt, but I'm praying by the end of this book we'll have something else in common too—the *hope* that comes from discovering God's faithfulness in the most unexpected places.

Your story, and the story of the child you lost too soon, isn't finished yet.

—Holley Gerth, author of the best-selling book
*Rain on Me: Devotions of Hope and Encouragement
for Difficult Times*, www.holleygerth.com

Introduction

No Broken Promises

hope for today ——————————————————

He has given us his very great and precious promises.

2 PETER 1:4

I promise. Each of us has likely uttered that phrase more times than we care to recall. In fact, if we're honest with ourselves, we've likely made such a vow quite recently. If we were to take inventory of our conversations in the past week, I bet we could call to mind several promises that we've made. Some of us may have made assurances to our husbands, our family members, our friends, or ourselves. Some of us may have even made commitments to God in prayer. These vows we've made could be anything from a simple, "I promise to do the laundry first thing in the morning," or "I promise to call you right back." On a more serious note, such promises could have looked something like, "Lord, I promise to turn away from my sin of _____." You fill in the blank.

By the same token, we've likely had others make promises to us. Perhaps you were the one who was promised to receive a call back.

13

Maybe a friend promised to meet you for coffee, or perhaps your husband made a promise to pray for a particular need you have in life right now.

Whatever the case, we can each relate to what it's like being both the giver and the receiver of a promise. In light of this, how many of us can say that we've never been the recipient of a broken promise? Sadly, I don't think one of us could make such a claim. Let's look inward. How many of us can declare that we've never broken a promise? As for me . . . guilty.

In my own experience as well as the experiences of the many women I have ministered to who have endured miscarriage or infant loss, I have found that people fail us over and over. *Can you relate?* We tend to place certain expectations on those who surround us—friends, relatives, and loved ones in particular. We expect that they will come alongside us and support us in our grief. We expect that they will have just the right words to say at just the right time. We expect them to know when to ask and when not to ask about our baby who died. We expect them to know when to hug, when to talk, and when to just sit and listen. We are full of expectations, promises of sorts, and sadly those around us fail to meet our expectations time and time again. Such failure lies in the very nature of our humanness. Let's admit it; we fail miserably at keeping promises, don't we? So how then can we expect any other human to fulfill the expectations we have at hand? The truth of the matter is that we can't.

I pose such questions not to be a discouragement, but to provide a basis for understanding the promises of God, particularly in light of our shared experience of loss. With God, there are no unmet expectations. He is fully capable and faithful to fulfill each and every promise He makes. The character of God is such that He cannot lie. Thus, if He makes a promise, we can trust that He will fulfill it. Let's take a look at a passage of Scripture from 2 Corinthians. In the apostle Paul's letter, we see a comparison between the words of men and the words of God:

Was I fickle when I intended to do this? Or do I make my plans in a worldly manner so that in the same breath I say both "Yes, yes" and "No, no"? But as surely as God is faithful, our message to you is not "Yes" and "No." For the Son of God, Jesus Christ, who was preached among you by us—by me and Silas and Timothy—was not "Yes" and "No," but in him it has always been "Yes." For no matter how many promises God has made, they are "Yes" in Christ. And so through him the "Amen" is spoken by us to the glory of God. (1:17–20)

Let me reiterate: "For no matter how many promises God has made, they are 'Yes' in Christ." What an encouragement to know that God's promises, however many He has made, are always, always, always a "Yes" in Christ! For those of us who belong to Him, who have put our faith and trust in Jesus, His promises are a "Yes!" And to that I say, Amen!

Let's turn our attention to another passage of Scripture that also addresses God's promises:

His divine power has given us everything we need for a godly life through our knowledge of him who called us by his own glory and goodness. Through these he has given us his very great and precious promises, so that through them you may participate in the divine nature, having escaped the corruption in the world caused by evil desires. (2 Peter 1:3–4)

God, in His unfathomable power, gives us everything we need! He is sufficient and His grace is enough. Still, if you're like me, you wrestle with the feelings of overwhelming grief after the loss of your precious baby. This is to be expected and you are not alone. Continue to walk through your grief one day at a time, at your own pace. Some of you may put unrealistic expectations on yourself to "be strong," as I have struggled with over the years. I caution you and urge you to remember that when we are weak, we are strong (2 Cor. 12:10) and we make our-selves ready for God to do His work, relying on His strength and not our own. Despite all the complexities of our grief, the heartbreaking loss of our baby, and the ugliness of the circumstances we find our-selves in, we're comforted by the fact that God has given us "very great and precious promises" (2 Peter 1:4). We will delve into these promises together in the pages to come.

How to Use This Book

Each chapter of this book focuses on a promise of God and is applied to the experience of miscarriage and infant loss. Woven throughout are aspects of my own stories of loss, as well as other women's stories. You will find "Hope for Today" Scripture verses interspersed throughout your reading and will also have opportunities for prayer, journaling, and a challenge to "Live it!"

verses to live by ——————————————————

His divine power has given us everything we need for a godly life through our knowledge of him who called us by his own glory and goodness.

2 PETER 1:3

For no matter how many promises God has made, they are "Yes" in Christ. And so through him the "Amen" is spoken by us to the glory of God.

2 CORINTHIANS 1:20

Before you begin, you will want to have a "Hope Journal" handy. This can be a notebook of your choosing, used for writing in response to the journal questions that are posed within the text of each chapter.

Whenever you are prompted, you should pause to journal your thoughts in your Hope Journal.

If you are working through this book in a small group format, leaders can find additional resources on the Mommies with Hope website at www.mommieswithhope.com. Mommies with Hope is a support group ministry for women who have experienced miscarriage and infant loss, based out of Central Iowa, providing biblically based support, both online as well as in face-to-face support group settings.

The Ultimate Promise

Before we delve deeper in the chapters to follow, let your mind wander with me for a moment. Rid yourself of any distraction and set aside the next few minutes as I guide you on an imaginary voyage. Give yourself permission to vividly capture each of the words below and picture them coming to life in your mind. Now, let's sail away . . .

Jesus, Our Life Preserver

Envision yourself drifting peacefully aboard a luxurious sailboat on the calm waters of the ocean. Crisp, white sails tower over you as you relax on the leather seating and take in the beauty of God's creation as the sun begins to set. Orange, yellow, and pink hues color the sky across the distance before you. The warm colors stretch the span of the ocean for what looks like eternity, as far as you can see from the east to the west. The horizon brings forth a sense of wonder and amazement as you marvel at the majesty of this moment. A gentle breeze wisps softly about you and rustles smoothly through your hair. The aroma of salty waters and the soothing sound of the sea calms your soul.

There is not a person or vessel in sight that could disrupt or detract from this miracle and you feel such a peace envelop you. Could it get any better than this?

Suddenly, storm clouds begin to roll in, seemingly out of nowhere. Darkness covers the sky and the once warm breeze begins to whip in winds of coldness that entirely engulf you. The shades of orange, yellow, and pink that once colored the canvas of the sky have made way for a dull gray, bringing in a sense of desolation as it drowns out any ray of sunlight that once peaked over the horizon. Without warning, the waves begin to rise and crash about in the seas. Icy rain begins to pour down, drenching every inch of your body. Every drop pricks like a needle, taunting you with a reminder of what once was, but never is to be again. Violent waves besiege you now as the waters begin to rush in, pouring over the edge of your once secure vessel. Within minutes, the sea floods your feet and ankles, rising to your knees and then your waist. Relentlessly, the waters encompass your body until you are nearly submerged. Numbness sets in and overtakes your entire being as the winds and rain continue to thrash all around. You feel completely alone, isolated and lost in the storm that surrounds you, which now seems to be mere background noise as you settle into a pit of despair.

As the waters rage, the vessel you once felt so safe and secure in continues to take in the sea. The weight of the water and the force of the winds shake any ounce of security you once held as the boat rocks violently amidst the crashing waves. Your knuckles turn white with fury as your hands clench on to anything they can grasp. You hang on for dear life to the boat that will soon give way to the powers of the sea. Your helpless cry is drowned by the storm. Pleas for rescue seem to be your only hope as you realize that there is nothing that can be done. You weep and wail as you fight for your life, outraged and confused by how suddenly circumstances have gone completely awry. A miracle is your only hope.

The sea has embraced you now as you struggle to stay afloat. You wonder how, and if, you will make it out of this storm alive. Your body is numb from the cold and shock of all that has occurred, yet your arms and legs flail to keep your head above water. You go through the motions, but in all reality, you are hopeless. Then, you spot it . . . the sailboat's life preserver. It must have come loose in the rush of the storm, and now it floats nearby, just beyond some debris from the boat's wreckage. It awaits your embrace, as you use all of your strength to swim for it. There is a glimmer of hope at the mere sight of this preserver. Your safety, your security, your salvation is within arm's reach. Your fingertips touch the edge of the preserver and confidence abounds as you are finally able to grasp the preserver with one whole hand, and now the other. You grab on and cling to the preserver with all the strength you can muster. Hope rushes in, just as quickly as the storm, as you rest in the safety of the life preserver, realizing that your decision to reach out and cling to the preserver was a matter of life and death.

hope for today ————————————————

My comfort in my suffering is this: Your promise preserves my life.

PSALM 119:50

Such a vision parallels my own loss experience. The beautiful sunset and peaceful seas remind me of the bliss I felt in knowing that we would be welcoming a child into this world. We had planned and hoped for more children, counting it a blessing that we were able to conceive quickly. Like you, we had hopes and dreams for our babies who now dwell in heaven. The horizon of these children's lives held endless possibilities. We anticipated a future full of the many joys children bring. The world seemed so right as we rejoiced and celebrated with expectation.

The storm began to set in when we received word that we, in fact, would not ever have the chance to parent our precious babies on this side of heaven. With our first daughter, Chloe Marie, it was the ultrasound diagnosis that revealed an "incompatible with life" prognosis. With the loss of our second baby, whom we later named Jesse, it was spontaneous bleeding and a call with the nurse practitioner confirming the worst. With our third loss, a baby girl named Riyah Mae, it was the silent sound of an absent heartbeat, verified in the same dreaded ultrasound room where we received the news of Chloe. Everything we had planned and hoped for came crashing down, right along with the waves in the sea of desperation that engulfed us. We saw no way out of the turmoil of grief that surrounded us, only darkness. It was cold and my arms were empty. I longed for my babies, each one of them, in ways I never knew possible. Each time, the news was unbearable. Each time, it hurt. Each loss was different, yet the pain was the same. The storms we faced had the propensity to sink us. At times, it felt as though an anchor was secured to my very heart, bringing me down into the abyss of the cold, black sea. A sea of empty. A sea of longing. A sea of heartache. A sea of pain. A sea of grief.

As we sank further into this sea of loss with our first child, some dear friends reached out and threw us a life preserver. When all hope seemed gone and we couldn't swim ourselves out of the storm that surrounded us, there was a glimmer of hope. The life preserver was within our reach. It kept us afloat and safe from harm. The fear and insecurity subsided as we clung to this life preserver. It rescued us from harm and brought us peace as it carried us back to shore. This life preserver saved us. This life preserver that I speak of has a name . . . Jesus. Jesus is within your reach. Jesus will keep you afloat and be your harbor of hope.

Jesus can wipe away any fear and insecurity if you would just cling to Him. Jesus will bring you to a place of peace. Jesus, and only Jesus, can completely save you. Together, through this study, we will seek and find as we reach for Him, Jesus, our life preserver.

hope for today ————————————————

You will seek me and find me when you seek me with all your heart.

JEREMIAH 29:13

———————————————————————

The promises of God are overwhelmingly abundant. Throughout His Word, God reveals His promises to us. He promises to never leave us or forsake us (Heb. 13:5), to be our refuge and shield (Ps. 18:2), to be our hiding place (Ps. 32:7), to be our portion (Ps. 73:26), and to give us abundant life in Christ (John 10:10). He promises us His love (1 John 4:16) and to give us hope and a future (Jer. 29:11). Most important of all, and because of His unfathomable love for us, He promises us eternity in heaven as we place our trust in Christ (John 3:16). Such promises bring great comfort for those of us who have endured suffering.

You have undoubtedly experienced suffering. Together, we mourn the loss of our babies. We grieve what might have been as we wonder about all our child would have done in life. Our plans for the future of our family no longer exist in the way that we had once imagined. We came to realize very quickly that the pain of loss, particularly the loss of a child, never goes away. While we cannot go back to how things once were or ever have our child back on this side of heaven, we can most assuredly rest in the promises of God.

Take some time to reflect and write in your Hope Journal in response to the questions posed below. Take an honest appraisal of your heart as you cope with your loss. As stated in Jeremiah 29:13, we will find when we seek with *all* our hearts.

pause to journal...

- ❧ If you haven't done so before, write out the story of your loss.
- ❧ If you could talk to God in person, what questions would you ask Him regarding your loss?
- ❧ In what ways has your loss been like a storm?
- ❧ What have you relied upon to be your "life preserver" in the storm of your loss?

Read through the words of your Hope Journal and reflect upon your story, your questions, your hurts, and who or what you have relied upon as your "life preserver." Think about what you would like to take away from completing this book, whether you are reading it on your own or as part of a group. Next, turn all of your thoughts and reflections into a personal prayer and write it in your Hope Journal.

pause to journal...

- ❧ What do you hope to learn as you read through this book in the shadow of your loss?
- ❧ Write your prayer.

My Prayer...

Heavenly Father, thank You for the blessing of all of my children, those living with me and those dwelling in Your presence. Thank You, especially, for Chloe, Jesse, and Riyah, as they have each taught me so much about life, love, and about being a mommy. Their brief lives have taught me about You too, God, and I'm so grateful. I admit, Lord, that it hurts so much to have endured these losses. With each pregnancy, I was hopeful and felt so blessed. Yet with each loss, my heart was torn into pieces and I questioned what Your plans were for my life. Through these losses, I have felt so completely alone and isolated at times, even though You have been here with me all along. Thank You for never leaving my side. I confess that I have relied on other people and things to help me get through. I've tried to be strong on my own over and over, but each time I fail and realize more and more my need to rely completely on You. You alone are sufficient. Help me, God, to trust only in You to see me through this storm. You alone are my life preserver. I pray that through looking at the promises found in Your Word, I come to know You more, Lord. Thank You, Father, for loving me and thank You for giving Your only Son, Jesus. It is in His precious name I pray. Amen.

Live It!

Knowing Jesus Christ as personal Savior is foundational to the rest of this book. If this is something you're unsure about, I want you to know that this free gift of salvation is offered to you today. Scripture tells us that today is the day of salvation (2 Cor. 6:2)! If you feel God tugging your heart toward repentance, pray and let Him in through trusting in Christ for the forgiveness of your sins, and be changed. Romans 10:9–10 says, "If you declare with your mouth, 'Jesus is Lord,' and believe in your heart that God raised him from the dead, you will be saved. For it is with your heart that you believe and are justified, and it is with your mouth that you profess your faith and are saved." (For more information on becoming a mommy with hope, please see appendix A.)

If you already know Christ as Savior, take some time to thank God for all He has done in your life. If you have questions you are wrestling with, pour them at Jesus' feet. First Peter 5:7 reminds us to cast our cares upon Him, Jesus, because He cares for us! Give it all to Him today, sister!

verses to live by ——————————————

My comfort in my suffering is this: Your promise preserves my life.

PSALM 119:50

❧ ❦

You will seek me and find me when you seek me with all your heart.

JEREMIAH 29:13

The Promise of His Love

hope for today ——————————————

And I pray that you, being rooted and established in love, may have power, together with all the Lord's holy people, to grasp how wide and long and high and deep is the love of Christ, and to know this love that surpasses knowledge—that you may be filled to the measure of all the fullness of God.

EPHESIANS 3:17–19

In the shadow of your grief, you may be wrestling with questions about God: His purpose, His love, and His willingness to allow such a thing to occur. After all, how could a loving God allow babies to die? If He truly loved us, wouldn't He spare us from such pain? Our human inclination is to ask these kinds of questions and long for the answers. In the wise words of a fellow mommy, pertaining to this very issue, "Answers would be good, though they will never do."

In all honesty, we may never find the answers we are seeking. I think back to the hours that followed the news of my most recent loss of Riyah Mae. I found myself in the living room of a precious friend's home. It was the only place I knew to go. Nicole greeted me at the door with tears in her eyes and immediately stretched out her arms to embrace me. Our bulging bellies touched each other as she held me in her doorway while I wailed. She was expecting too, due just a couple of weeks before me. Soon, our pastor arrived to be with us. I remember him saying, "Some things we may never have the answers to on this side of heaven." I knew this to be true and had verbalized it myself many times. I believed it then and I believe it now. The response that spewed forth in the midst of my grief, however, was, "Well, I am going to have *a lot* of questions for God when I get to heaven!"

After all, this was my third baby who had gone to be with Him. Hadn't I been through enough? Hadn't He taught me enough about this whole grief thing? It seems silly now, because I know that when I get to heaven, there will be no need for questioning. The painful reality of this fallen world will be vanquished for eternity. But for now, the questions remain and the answers seem elusive. God's Word may not give us the answers to all of our questions, but it does reveal to us the depth of God's love. A love that we need. A love we can trust. A love we must experience in order to embark on a journey of understanding.

hope for today ————————————————————

Let the morning bring me word of your unfailing love, for I have put my trust in you. Show me the way I should go, for to you I entrust my life.

PSALM 143:8

Love Before Birth

It seems obvious to state that as mothers we possess a love for our children that exists before birth. We have hopes, dreams, and plans for these little ones—oftentimes before receiving confirmation of their expected arrival. It's this love before birth that allows us to grieve at any stage of loss. Not only do we grieve the loss of the person they are, but we also grieve all that we dreamed they would become. Grief exists only because of the presence of a real, true, and meaningful love; a natural love that we have for our children, born or unborn. While we may never fully understand the enormity of God's love, I believe that a mother's love for her child is as close to an earthly parallel that our human hearts or minds could fathom. Even then, the comparison seems feeble.

Psalm 139 speaks of God's intimate knowledge of each one of us, His creation. It starts out with the psalmist, David, acknowledging that the God of the universe knows him in ways that no one could. He knows me too, and fellow mommy, He knows you. Verses 1–6 read:

> You have searched me, LORD,
>   and you know me.
> You know when I sit and when I rise;
>   you perceive my thoughts from afar.
> You discern my going out and my lying down;
>   you are familiar with all my ways.
> Before a word is on my tongue
>   you, LORD, know it completely.
> You hem me in behind and before,
>   and you lay your hand upon me.
> Such knowledge is too wonderful for me,
>   too lofty for me to attain.

Do you believe it? The God of all creation knows you. He really knows you. As Creator, He loves all that He has created; this includes you and the precious life that grew within you, for however brief a time.

Take some time to read through verses 13–16 of Psalm 139, where David confidently proclaims:

For you created my inmost being;
   you knit me together in my mother's womb.
I praise you because I am fearfully and wonderfully made;
   your works are wonderful,
   I know that full well.
My frame was not hidden from you
   when I was made in the secret place,
   when I was woven together in the depths of the earth.
Your eyes saw my unformed body;
   all the days ordained for me were written in your book
   before one of them came to be.

Let's not gloss over these verses, ladies. There are some powerful truths packed into this portion of Scripture that are worthy of reflecting upon.

pause to journal . . .

ৡ What truths do you see in Psalm 139? What is your reaction to these truths?

ৡ In what ways can you apply the truths of these verses to your personal experience of loss?

ৡ What does Psalm 139:13–16 mean to you in relation to your loss experience?

A Selfless Love

True love is selfless. Selflessness is demonstrated as concern for others' welfare or desires over one's own. While sitting in my favorite coffee shop, I witnessed a simple example of such selflessness. A young mother was out with her two children, a boy and a girl who looked to be about two and four years old, respectively. In the middle of this quaint café, the siblings ran back and forth across the beaten wood floor as their mother attempted to reprimand. The pitter-patter of their hustling little feet was a distraction to some, yet caused a smile to stretch across my face. Eagerly, the children wandered toward the gumball machine and soon the clacking and cranking of the gears resounded as the young ones awaited their treat. Next, the gumball rolled down the metal pipeline, gaining momentum, only to drop to the floor below. The sound of the gumball hitting the floor caused me to turn my head with curiosity as to what this hurried mom would do next. I grinned when I saw her lick the gumball before passing it along to her little girl. Something only a mother would do—wash away the germs to protect her child. I just smiled. I can't say I endorse the effectiveness of this method. But I get it, and I bet you do too. Only the selfless love of a mother would cause a grown woman to lick a gumball clean from a café's dirty floor!

Together, we could think of many more examples of a mother's selfless love—serving herself last at dinner each night, sacrificing hours of sleep to nurse her hungry child, or going without in order to provide. This is what mothers do. It is a natural selflessness rooted in the love she has for her children. Now, think about this: could a mother love her child so much that she'd give up her very life? I believe so. But what about this: could you imagine a mother giving her child's life to save someone else? What if that someone else were her enemy? It seems senseless, right? However, this is precisely what God did for you, for me, and for each of our precious babies who are with Him now. He gave us His Son, Jesus. He gave up His Son's life. That is how much He loves us.

hope for today ———————————

For God so loved the world that he gave his one and only Son, that whoever believes in him shall not perish but have eternal life.

JOHN 3:16

Selfless to Sacrificial

The truth that God gave up His Son for us extends far beyond a mere selfless act of love. This act of love demonstrated for you, for me, for our babies, and for all the world is the ultimate example of God's *sacrificial* love. Those of us who've experienced the death of a baby know the pain of loss and the reality of grief. Can you imagine sending your child to face a horrendous death for the sake of a bunch of sinners? I realize the question seems absurd! Yet God experienced grief and loss willingly because He loves us. Romans 5:8 explains, "God demonstrates his own love for us in this: While we were still sinners, Christ died for us." He sent His Son as a demonstration of His love, even "while we were still sinners." First John 3:16 provides us a definition of love that says, "This is how we know what love is: Jesus Christ laid down his life for us." God gave His Son so that we may be called His children. What an amazing truth to be thankful for today as we contemplate the promise of God's love. First John 4:10 defines love in a similar way: "This is love: not that we loved God, but that he loved us and sent his Son as an atoning sacrifice for our sins." God initiates the relationship by loving us first. It is His immense love and grace that enable us to come into a saving relationship with Him through Christ.

A fellow mommy, Kimberlee, who follows the *Mommies with Hope* blog, commented on a post about God's sacrificial love shortly after her daughter, Lulu, died. She shared her heart as she realized the magnitude of His love:

> Today I spent time with God crying in my hurt of not having my baby in my arms, not seeing her have a head of hair. And then I read 1 John and finally, for the first time in my life, I got it. I.GOT.IT. I have gone to church all my life, I have always felt I didn't have a story, a powerful testimony. And I think of the Scripture of those [who] love much who have been forgiven much. And of course, I am a sinner, and Jesus died for me, I get all that. But [more so] after reading 1 John and reading that we are called chil-

dren of God because He loves us. I love my children, both living and dead, and long to have known my daughter who is with Him. And it hurts so deep. But God's love for me, for us, is deeper! And it took losing a child to get that. To finally get it. I have learned the most bittersweet lesson of all. . . . To not just know His love, but to experience it. How deep, how wide, how long, and how high it is! It's freeing and powerful and overwhelming. I was drowning in quicksand of sadness and hurt but now I am drowning in His love. And I have let go, to float on the waves. It's a freeing feeling to let go and get lost in the ocean of His love. The thorn I will always have is the loss of Lulu, of a baby I never got to know, but got to hold for a while. And His thorn brings peace and love in the hurt of my thorn. I will never have to feel the crown of thorns He wore for me, but I will always have a reminder of the pain He suffered just for me. In all my life of being His child, I finally get what it costs. Today! What His love feels like! Makes me want to shout it from a mountaintop! I now have a story, and don't they all come with a cost?

hope for today

See what great love the Father has lavished on us, that we should be called children of God! And that is what we are!

1 JOHN 3:1

pause to journal . . .

- What is your reaction to Kimberlee's thoughts about God's love, as written above?
- In what ways is your own experience similar? In what ways is it different?
- How has God shown you His love in the shadow of your loss?

hope for today —————————————————————————

For you died, and your life is now hidden with Christ in God.

COLOSSIANS 3:3

_____

Whose We Are

In the years since my losses, I've learned much about who I am. I admit that all too often I've allowed circumstances, roles, and achievements to serve as the definition of my identity. If given the task of making a list in response to the question, "Who are you?" my typical response may look something like this:

wife

mom

bereaved parent

support group leader

sister

daughter

aunt

teacher

leader

Christian

author

speaker

friend

And the list goes on . . . each item an indication of the many roles I fill in life: some familial, others social, and still others occupational. What would your list look like?

&ed; Who are you? Make a list of your various roles and describe them in your Hope Journal.

While there is value in knowing who I am in relation to the various roles I fill (wife, mom, daughter, friend, etc.), I've learned that it is abundantly more important to possess security in knowing *whose* I am. May others see me as a beloved daughter of the King. More importantly, may *I* know that is who I am, and He is who I belong to! First John 3:1 says, "See what great love the Father has lavished on us, that we should be called children of God! And that is what we are!" Once we begin to realize whose we are, we can rest securely in the loving arms of our Father.

King David of the Old Testament was a man who rested in the security of God's love. In Psalm 17, David approaches God with confidence:

> I call on you, my God, for you will answer me;
> turn your ear to me and hear my prayer.
> Show me the wonders of your great love,
> you who save by your right hand
> those who take refuge in you from their foes.
> Keep me as the apple of your eye;
> hide me in the shadow of your wings. (Ps. 17:6–8)

May these words be an example to live by in how we ought to approach our loving God. They were penned for each one of us. His Word is His love letter to us. He wants you and me to come before Him as David did—to trust that He will answer us when we call upon Him, that He will save us as we take refuge in Him, and that you and I are the apple of His eye.

It is my deepest desire that you experience God's love in the shadow of your loss. God's love is unlike any earthly love we could ever experience or imagine. His abiding love is always with us, unending and permanent. God has assured us, "Never will I leave you; never will I forsake you" (Heb. 13:5). God's love never fails. Never. His love is available to all. Just as God is the I Am, so is His love. It just is. Because God is love.

hope for today ————————————————

We love because he first loved us.

1 JOHN 4:19

My Prayer for You, Fellow Mommy . . .

Lord, thank You for being a God who is all-loving, even in the midst of heartache and pain. You have made Your love known to us through Your Son, Jesus. Thank You for Your sacrificial love, demonstrated by Jesus' death on the cross. I pray that this woman would feel and experience Your love as she lives in the shadow of loss. Be with her throughout her days, Lord, revealing Your love to her in big ways and small. Lord, help her to understand the depth of Your everlasting, unfailing, faithful, trustworthy, and saving love. Amen.

Live It!

In your Hope Journal, write two love letters:

- Address one of the letters to your baby (or babies), expressing your hopes, dreams, and love for him or her. Share your heart about who you thought they would become.
- The second letter should be a love letter to *yourself* from God. Write the message that you think He would want to share with

you today as you live in His love. Consider reading it when you experience a tough day ahead.

verses to live by ──────────────

Your eyes saw my unformed body; all the days ordained for me were written in your book before one of them came to be.

PSALM 139:16

❧ ☙

See what great love the Father has lavished on us, that we should be called children of God! And that is what we are!

1 JOHN 3:1

❧ ☙

And I pray that you, being rooted and established in love, may have power, together with all the Lord's holy people, to grasp how wide and long and high and deep is the love of Christ, and to know this love that surpasses knowledge—that you may be filled to the measure of all the fullness of God.

EPHESIANS 3:17–19

The Promise of His Goodness

hope for today ——————————————

Give thanks to the LORD, for he is good; his love endures forever.

PSALM 118:29

"What could possibly be *good* about the death of a baby?" This was a question posed to me by a former student. Having previously taught an infant development course at the university level, I have been afforded many opportunities to share my story of Chloe's prenatal diagnosis and subsequent death as it related to the course content. Each time, the story changed. I emphasized some aspects of the story more than others, depending on where I was in my grief journey. In the beginning, the sequence of events was most important for me to share, as I divulged every detail, fact, and piece of information in chronological fashion. Over time, I changed. More accurately stated, God changed me. As He worked in and through my grief, the perception of my experience and sharing of the story changed too. In every telling, I was and am prompted to share my view of God's blessings as well as the reality of His presence. Always.

In any case, this student of mine had learned about Chloe. It impacted her and she was inspired to tell a friend. The question posed above, "What could possibly be *good* about the death of a baby?" was her friend's response, which she later conveyed to me. My reply? It's a matter of perspective. The focus must shift from the circumstances to the Savior. Of course there is nothing good about the death of a baby. However, He is good, even when babies die.

When a woman struggles to become pregnant month after month, longing for a child, He is good. In the anticipation at the sight of a positive pregnancy test, He is good. In the shadows of disappointment with no hope for pregnancy in sight, He is good. In the ultrasound room, where parents meet their child face-to-face with joyful expectation, He is good. In that same ultrasound room, when the silence of no heartbeat abounds, when a flat line pierces your soul, and when the hopeful dreams you had for your child die alongside his or her tiny body, He, our God, is still good. Though our circumstances in the midst of the heartbreaking reality of loss are far from good, God is always good. Always. That is the reliable, dependable, unchanging nature of who He is. James 1:17 reminds us: "Every good and perfect gift is from above, coming down from the Father of the heavenly lights, who does not change like shifting shadows." Our children, no matter how briefly they lived, were and are a gift from God; our God who *does not change.*

hope for today ─────────────────────

And we know that in all things God works for the good of those who love him, who have been called according to his purpose.

ROMANS 8:28

All Things for Good?

Not only is our God a good God, but He also works all things for good. All things? Yes. Even the death of a baby. An array of dismal feelings and thoughts bubble to the surface and linger as we trudge through the grief. We question: How could a good God allow such suffering? Why would God take my baby, yet allow another baby to be born into an abusive home? Why does this woman in the supermarket even have children if she only wishes to yell and yank them around?"

These are tough questions for which we may never have answers. We can, however, realign our thinking to delve into an understanding of the goodness of God, despite the looming questions and difficult circumstances. Let's be honest—questions such as these fail to give us a true sense of peace. Rather, they may pave the way for bitterness to take root in our hearts. Psalm 73:21–22 reads, "When my heart was grieved and my spirit embittered, I was senseless and ignorant; I was a brute beast before you." Can you relate? Senseless. Ignorant. A brute beast. I realize these aren't the most uplifting of words. Yet, let's examine ourselves by asking the following questions in response to these verses.

pause to journal . . .

> What has been my typical reaction toward God in the shadow of my loss?
> Have I turned toward Him or away from Him?
> Have I become a bitter person? How?

Your response to the questions posed above may expose some things of which you are not proud. At least that has been the case for me at certain points along my grief journey. The good news is that we serve a God who knows our hearts, even the ugliest and most embittered parts and pieces, and He loves us anyway.

I pray you find comfort in the encouraging verses that follow, as the psalmist goes on to say, "Yet I am always with you; you hold me by my right hand. You guide me with your counsel, and afterward you will take me into glory" (Ps. 73:23–24). Let us not merely skim over these words. His words. Swallow these words and digest them as you reflect on His promise. His goodness. Psalm 34:8 reminds us, "Taste and see that the LORD is good; blessed is the one who takes refuge in him." God is with you. He holds your right hand. He guides you with His counsel. One day, He will usher you into His glory. We serve a good God, fellow mommies! Psalm 73 concludes with these faith-filled words:

> Whom have I in heaven but you?
>   And earth has nothing I desire besides you.
> My flesh and my heart may fail,
>   but God is the strength of my heart
>   and my portion forever.
> Those who are far from you will perish;
>   you destroy all who are unfaithful to you.
> But as for me, it is good to be near God.
>   I have made the Sovereign LORD my refuge;
>   I will tell of all your deeds. (vv. 25–28)

pause to journal . . .

 Reread Psalm 73:25–28. Reflect upon these Scriptures and examine your heart. Say each word, speaking it to the Lord God directly in prayer. Consider the following questions as a part of your prayer:

God, are You my only desire on this earth?

God, are You the strength of my heart?

God, are You near? Am I seeking You?

God, are You my refuge?

⁞ God already knows the honest answers to these questions. Still, we ask them in order to reveal the truth about the attitude of our hearts. What truths did this exercise reveal to you? Write your thoughts in your Hope Journal.

⁞ Which of the verses from this passage resonates with you most? Explain.

⁞ Verse 28 of this passage asserts, "it is good to be near God." In what ways have you felt near to God in the midst of your grief?

⁞ In what ways have you seen God "work all things for good" in your life? Consider past experiences or circumstances where you have seen His handiwork.

hope for today —————————————————————

Taste and see that the LORD is good; blessed is the one who takes refuge in him.

PSALM 34:8

_____

Good Grief

Good grief—an expression used often in our society. If we're honest, we have likely uttered this phrase ourselves. But what does it even mean? Can grief really be good? We use phrases such as this so innocently in an effort to avoid saying something harsh. I am guilty a hundred times over with expressions like, oh my goodness, goodness gracious, holy moly, and the list goes on. In fact, when my son was four years old, he picked up on one of my catchy little phrases. It was summertime and he was attending his first-ever vacation Bible school. Midway through the week, we were on our way to vacation Bible school and I decided to quiz him about the topic under study for that day—the Trinity. I asked him, "Can you tell me the three parts of the Trinity?" He responded proudly with a hint of hesitation, "God, the Father." "And?" I questioned. "Jesus," he continued. Beaming, I was proud of my sweet boy learning all about his God. I interrupted the long pause to prompt him to share the third part of the Trinity by saying, "And what's the third, Gabe?" With a quizzical look upon his face, as though he was only partly sure of his answer, he replied in a questioning tone, "The holy moly?" True story. Not one of my proudest moments, but a moment when he taught me a lesson about the words that freely spew forth from my lips.

Another commonly used expression is the phrase "good God." In the correct context these are great words. In frustration, these words contradict God's very command found in Exodus 20:7, which clearly states: "You shall not misuse the name of the LORD your God, for the LORD will not hold anyone guiltless who misuses his name." This is straightforward, so I will spare you the sermonette regarding the *misuse* of God's name. And never mind the mere fact that this very verse is one of the Ten Commandments! I do, however, want us to spend some time reflecting upon the *majesty* of His name.

There are numerous names for God in the Bible. Authors write entire books devoted to the names of God. His names provide insight into His character and the truth about who He is. Each of His names reveals a bit more about His promises. The name of God, Jehovah Rapha, means "the Lord is Healer." *How has He provided a sense of healing to your hurting soul in the shadow of your loss?* Another of His names, El Elyon, translates to "Most High God." *Do you believe that He is "Most High"? Sovereign over all? That He has a purpose in and through this?* Jehovah Shammah means "the Lord is there." The truth of Scripture supports that God is everywhere. In Ezekiel 48:35 where this particular name of God is used, the Scripture is referring to an actual, physical place. Heaven. He is there, and our babies are with Him in His dwelling place. *Does this bring you comfort? Do you have full assurance that you will join them one day?* El Shaddai, translated as "the Lord Almighty," reminds us yet again that our God reigns supreme. His might is unquestionable. *Do you believe it?* I reflect upon these few names of God and cannot help but see the promise of His goodness burst forth. Our God is the God who heals, He is Most High, He is seated on the throne, and He reigns with power and might! To say that God is good is likely the most enormous understatement of the century. He is more than good and so far above the earthly trials we face.

hope for today

I will proclaim the name of the LORD. Oh, praise the greatness of our God!

DEUTERONOMY 32:3

A Good God—Still and Always

Grief is not good, yet my God sure is—still and always and forever will be. When we can cry out in our grief, "good God!" and mean it as an outcry of faith, we are on the path to truly understanding His goodness. Such understanding extends beyond the circumstances, beyond the heartache, beyond the pain. Is grief good? No. But my God, who walks me through my grief, is always good. The ability to believe and proclaim God's goodness in the midst of grief is truly a measure of faith. It's being able to say and believe, "He's still my God" when grief settles deep within our souls. Still and always and forever will be.

I want to share with you the story of a couple who exemplified this kind of faith in the midst of their grief. Much like our experience with Chloe, this couple faced a decision that no parents should ever have to make. Midway through their pregnancy, Darin and Deanna received confirmation that their unborn son, Noah, had a kidney condition that was incompatible with life. They chose to continue the pregnancy with Noah, knowing that he would die shortly after birth. I've been blessed by talking with them about their experience, as they demonstrate a faith that centers on God's goodness, despite the overwhelming grief.

During the weeks and months that spanned the remainder of their pregnancy with Noah, Darin and Deanna's family and friends made it known that they were petitioning the Lord for the miraculous healing of Noah. He certainly was able. He is the God over all; all-powerful, all-knowing, and all-loving. They believed God could do a miracle. What stood out to me, however, was the fact that they resolved to love God even if He did not heal their boy. Noah was born in May of 2004 and went to be with Jesus within an hour of his birth. From the world's perspective, there was no miracle. God did not physically heal him as some had hoped and prayed. Yet I would venture to proclaim that Noah experienced the ultimate healing touch of our Savior as he was ushered into heaven and experienced the greatest miracle of all: God's loving mercy.

When Darin and Deanna share their story, they refer to the account of Shadrach, Meshach, and Abednego found in Daniel 3 from the Old Testament. In summary, King Nebuchadnezzar appointed three wise men to oversee the province of Babylon, under the recommendation of Daniel, who had previously revealed and interpreted the king's mysterious dream. King Nebuchadnezzar was astounded by Daniel's interpretation of his dream, which Daniel considered to be a vision from God. Shortly after the king had made these appointments, he created an idol in the form of a gold statue, measuring ninety feet high and nine feet wide, as this was a part of his dream. He commanded everyone to fall to their knees in worship of the statue at the sound of various instruments. Those who did not obey this command, according to King Nebuchadnezzar, would be thrown into a fiery furnace to face certain death. Shadrach, Meshach, and Abednego refused to follow such a command because they knew and loved the one and only God, our Father. When the king received word of their refusal to bow down and worship the gold statue that he had created, he confronted the three wise men and threatened them with his warning. In response to his threat to toss them in the blazing furnace, Shadrach, Meshach, and Abednego boldly responded by saying,

> King Nebuchadnezzar, we do not need to defend ourselves before you in this matter. If we are thrown into the blazing furnace, the God we serve is able to deliver us from it, and he will deliver us from Your Majesty's hand. But even if he does not, we want you to know, Your Majesty, that we will not serve your gods or worship the image of gold you have set up. (Dan. 3:16–18)

In other words, they were saying . . .

>> Our God is able to save us.

>> Our God will save us.

>>> But even if He does not . . . He is still our God!

Thus was the heart of Darin and Deanna as they faced the reality of Noah's impending death. In Philippians 4:13 the apostle Paul proclaims, "I can do all this through him who gives me strength." I believe that this Christ-centered faith is precisely what gave Darin and Deanna the strength to believe and proclaim that they worship the God who is able to heal and save in miraculous ways, yet love Him even when He chooses not to. As for Shadrach, Meshach, and Abednego, they were tossed into that fiery furnace, as King Nebuchadnezzar had promised. In faith, God protected them from sure destruction, as each of them remained unscathed. What's more, the king and his counselors gazed upon the fiery furnace and they saw four individuals inside, rather than three. In Daniel 3:25, King Nebuchadnezzar says, "Look! . . . I see four men loose, walking in the midst of the fire; and they are not hurt, and the form of the fourth is like the Son of God" (NKJV). Can you imagine peering into that blazing furnace and viewing such a sight? Jesus was walking with them in the midst of that fire! They saw Jesus, and His power was made known by the evidence that

Shadrach, Meshach, and Abednego walked through the fire and into safety unharmed. This truly was a miracle. It was their faith that saved them, physically. Yet their faith ran deeper still in that they knew and worshiped the God who was worthy of praise regardless of whether He unveiled His cloak of protection. They had chosen to believe in their God either way and only proved themselves right when God showed up strong. You may begin to wonder: *Why didn't God show up and save my child?* This is a good and honest question, one that will be addressed in further detail when we delve into the promise of His purpose in the next chapter. The crux of the answer lies in a truth from Scripture that we have already begun to examine—our God works *all* things for good; this work is always in line with His purpose. Fellow mommy, you must know, God was never absent. He was, is, and always will be there.

Loving God and recognizing His goodness when life doesn't go according to our plan is a difficult task, unattainable by our own strength. It is Christ within us who allows us to praise God in the storms of this life. Just as He was with Shadrach, Meshach, and Abednego in the fiery furnace, He was with Darin and Deanna throughout the course of their pregnancy with Noah. He walked alongside them every step of the way. He was with me in the midst of my own fiery furnace of grief and He is with you too.

hope for today ————————————————————

Surely goodness and mercy shall follow me all the days of my life; and I will dwell in the house of the LORD forever.

PSALM 23:6 NKJV

Below is an excerpt from the *Mommies with Hope* blog, written two days after the loss of my youngest daughter, Riyah Mae. Looking back, I can see how God prepared me for the news in that ultrasound room and how Christ, who lives in me, gave me the strength to truly believe that He was and is and forever will be good.

November 7, 2009

On Thursday morning, I went to the doctor. Some of you know this, while others of you did not . . . we were expecting again. In fact, we had just started to spread the news in the last couple of weeks or so. After all we had reached that magic number—twelve weeks. I had already had blood work and two ultrasounds and things were progressing wonderfully. So going to the doctor on Thursday morning was just another part of my day. I got the kids off to school, Justin went to work, I talked to my mom on the phone on the way down, etc. I had a busy day ahead of me, needing to get back to Ames to give an exam to my class that afternoon and attend Gabe's conference later that night. Just another ordinary day. But God, in His perfect sovereignty and will, had other plans in store for us that day. It calls to mind Proverbs 16:9, which says, "In their hearts humans plan their course, but the LORD establishes their steps."

In the office, my nurse was going to take a listen to the heartbeat. We both knew that sometimes it can be hard to find the heartbeat with those Doppler wands and that if we couldn't find it, I would get in for a quick ultrasound to *see* the baby's heartbeat—even better! She couldn't find it on the Doppler, but left the room unconcerned to see who could do the ultrasound to show the heartbeat. As I sat in that exam room alone, for truly just a minute or so, I took the time to talk to God. I remember distinctly saying to God, over and over, "Whatever happens, I will still love You. I will still love You. I will still love You." Next thing I know, I was in the ultrasound room with my nurse,

Emily (the sonographer, a student of mine who I've come to know so well).

So I laid back, eager to see the images overhead. With just a few glimpses, Emily sorrowfully had to say, "Teske, I don't see a heartbeat." Then, the tears. The wailing. The confusion. I didn't understand. I don't understand. And quite honestly, I don't know if I will ever understand. But I remembered those words that I had prayed to God, just moments before, and I meant them with all my heart. "I will still love You, God." What's more, I will still serve You. I will still praise Your Name. I will still give my life to You. I will still glorify You. I will still trust in You. You are still my God.

My Prayer for You, Fellow Mommy . . .

Lord, I know that You are good. I have seen and experienced Your goodness in my life in countless ways, but confess that I sometimes fail to recognize it. I pray, Lord, that during these times of grief when life seems so unfair, when we have a hard time understanding, grasping, and embracing Your goodness, that You would bring a peace and a comfort to this woman who is seeking Your goodness. Help her to trust You, Father. Work in her heart so that she may see Your goodness in all things—even in the shadow of her loss. In Your perfect timing, Lord, reveal to this woman the ways in which You are working all things for good. Your Word tells us that You have a plan and a purpose for this fellow mommy and for her baby's life. I pray that You will use this for good, even if she can't even begin to see what that may look like as I cry out to You on her behalf. Your love endures forever! Amen.

Live It!

In your Hope Journal, make a list of the ways in which you have experienced God's goodness. These can be things from your past as well as your current situation. Spend some time reflecting on your list and thanking God for His goodness in your life.

verses to live by ──────────────

Give thanks to the LORD, for he is good; his love endures forever.

PSALM 118:29

⋐§ ⋑

I will proclaim the name of the LORD. Oh, praise the greatness of our God!

DEUTERONOMY 32:3

4

The Promise of His Purpose

hope for today ────────────

"For I know the plans I have for you," declares the LORD, "plans to prosper you and not to harm you, plans to give you hope and a future."

JEREMIAH 29:11

If we're honest, each of us could admit that we like to have some sense of control over our circumstances. Early on in life we make plans. As young children, we plan our day, filling the hours with crafty projects, outdoor activities, and sweet indulgences at the acquiescence of our parents. When things don't go according to plan, tensions rise and, worst-case scenario, tantrums ensue. During our teenage years, it's all about friends and fun, as we contemplate how we will spend our weekends and with whom we will attend the prom. Inevitably, we consider our futures, as one chapter of our lives concludes and the commencement of adulthood emerges. First loves, broken hearts, and real-world hurts. So marks the beginning of the reality that things don't always go as we plan.

As Jeremiah 29:11 asserts, God has a plan and purpose for each of our lives. Yes, we may know all too well the pain of a broken heart and the reality of this fallen world. The truth, however, is that God's plans are to prosper, not to harm; to give a future and a hope—even in the midst of our brokenness.

Shattered Dreams

Somewhere along the way, we've each come to the point in life where children enter the scene. For most of you, children were a part of the plan from the start. Still others may find themselves in the trenches of loss after an unplanned pregnancy. In either scenario, plans derail and grief runs deep. Through tears, Nicole shared with me the story of her miscarriage, which occurred at fourteen weeks gestation. She talked in-depth about the dismissing attitude of those who surrounded her and how such sentiments starkly contrasted the emotion she felt in the aftermath of her loss. After all, being a mommy was a dream of hers since childhood. She reminisced on her days as a little girl, the season when this dream took root, with hopes of blossoming into a growing family. She reflects now on her adulthood reality, severed by the pain of mourning a baby who was gone too soon; a pain dismissed by so many, yet all too real to those of us who have "been there."

The grief we experience in the shadow of miscarriage or infant loss is a complex grief. Not only do we grieve the loss of the person, our precious child who mattered and meant something, but we also grieve what *should* have been. We had plans for our children. We had hopes for who they would become. When the death of a baby occurs, so too does the death of a dream; a dream so often rooted in our hearts from the days of our own girlhood adventures, as was the case for Nicole.

ह≫ When did you first know you wanted to be a mommy?
ह≫ How has your view or experience of motherhood been impacted by
   your loss?

Our Plans

I think back to that whirlwind of a day, ultrasound day, February 16, 2006. It was like any other day in our everyday lives, hurried and busy. It was late winter in Iowa, thus complete with a snowstorm, delaying our already rushed schedule as we raced across town to make it to our appointment. Though flustered, we were excited. I remember the relief of making it to the office on time, checking in with a video camera in hand, anxious to capture the images of our baby on camera. Within minutes, we were called back to the exam room. I didn't know it was a girl at the time, as we had *planned* on being surprised. That would change all too soon. We met our baby in that ultrasound room: our baby who, to us, looked absolutely perfect. We saw her profile. We saw her tiny hands and feet and watched her little heart beat at a steady pace. We heard the continual, reassuring tones resound loudly as the cool touch of the wand glided across my swelling tummy. It was the sound of life, precious moments, and the start of a new and exciting beginning for us. I met my daughter in the exam room that day with eager anticipation and a curiosity for who she would become. I carried with me the hopes and dreams for a future life together.

By this time in the pregnancy, we'd already told our son, Gabe, then a tender-hearted four-year-old, that he would be a big brother. We had plans for picnic outings and swimming pool debuts, as she was due to be born in early July. Oh, can't you just imagine how precious our baby girl would've looked in a tiny ruffled swimsuit, donning a sun hat and shades? We promised Gabe that he could help feed her and be our special helper. These were our plans. Silly and trivial, yet the mark of our normal, everyday lives. What we've learned along the way, however, is that God's purpose is always greater than our human plans.

hope for today

"For my thoughts are not your thoughts, neither are your ways my ways," declares the LORD. "As the heavens are higher than the earth, so are my ways higher than your ways and my thoughts than your thoughts."

ISAIAH 55:8–9

His plans are always far better than anything we could have imagined for ourselves. Six years ago, I couldn't have imagined that the situation we faced would be comprised of any good. Little did I know that God would reveal more of the story in the months and years that followed and I can honestly say that I wouldn't trade any of it.

Our Reality

All too soon, we realized that life—her life, our lives—would not go on how *we* had planned. The daydreaming and steady reverie of her budding life would be cut short with these piercing words: "Your baby has a problem. Your baby is going to die." Die? Die! Yes, die. Hearing those words produced a wave of desperation that washed over me unlike anything I've ever felt. It was as if someone had reached their hand into the center of my chest and tore my heart clean out from my body. The pain was indescribable. It felt like I was literally heartbroken. Tears. Wailing. Longing. Pain. Shock. Numbness. Disgust. It couldn't be true. Yet it was. Our plans had gone awry, as our reality set in. There would be no summer picnics or days at the pool. No big brother bottle-feedings or special-helper tasks. No father-daughter dances or princess birthday parties. No senior prom, and no wedding day. Gone were the dreams we had for our baby girl. Gone in an instant, swallowed up in the ugly moments of that dreaded ultrasound room. The dreams we once held were forever washed away in the reality of impending death.

Still, there is comfort in the truth that the news of her diagnosis did not take God by surprise. In our previous study of Psalm 139, we heard David proclaim, "Your eyes saw my unformed body; all the days ordained for me were written in your book before one of them came to be" (v. 16). Yes, the Creator God knew her days. Did I wish for more time? Certainly! Yet I have learned that it is better to trust God than to rely on my own longings and desires. After all, He loved her more than I ever could.

It has been a long road, but one that I would travel again, knowing now that there is blessing on the other side. The pain has been unrelenting at times, but is nothing compared to the joy of knowing how the story of her brief life has brought glory to the King. This is the testimony to His faithfulness. He is a Redeemer of all things and I have seen firsthand how *His plans* are far better than anything I could imagine.

---

pause to journal . . .

ૐ What plans did you have for your baby?
ૐ What was your reality?

hope for today ————————————————

There is a time for everything, and a season for every activity under the heavens: . . . a time to weep and a time to laugh, a time to mourn and a time to dance.

ECCLESIASTES 3:1, 4

Everything Happens for a Reason . . . blah, blah, blah

"Everything happens for a reason."

"There must be some purpose behind this."

"God has a plan."

"This is probably for the better."

Unfortunately, it's likely that you have heard these statements a time or two in the aftermath of your loss. In fact, these very words may have flowed freely from your own mouth, either as you have told others about your experience, or have sought meaning and purpose in the pain. These aren't necessarily *bad* statements to make; neither are they false. From a biblical perspective, there is some truth to each one . . . we will get to that in a moment. Sometimes, though, the mere sound of such statements can sting, however laden with truth they may be. The reality of our experience is that it hurts. Our hearts ache in ways we never thought possible. Tears flow freely, just when we thought there were no tears left to cry.

The biblical truth to grasp and cling to is that God truly does have a plan and purpose in store for you *and* your baby. Consider Job from the Bible. Job was a godly man, proved righteous by his faith. Calamities struck his household, his family, his livelihood, and his health. Friends offered no real sense of support and even Job described them as "miserable comforters" (Job 16:2). He remained faithful to God, trusting that there was purpose in his pain. Eventually, Job questions God—a typical *Why do bad things happen to good people?* approach. God turns the questioning right back at Job, starting with these words: "Who is this that obscures my plans with words without knowledge? Brace yourself like a man; I will question you, and you shall answer me" (38:2–3). Yikes! Then, after a whopping 101 verses in Scripture of God turning the tables on Job, Job humbly replies, "I know that you can do all things; no purpose of yours can be thwarted. You asked, 'Who is this that obscures my plans without knowledge?' Surely I spoke of things I did not understand, things too wonderful for me to know" (42:2–3).

Job understood that God's ways were bigger than our own. He trusted that God had his best in mind, even if the circumstances suggested the opposite.

God's divine plans are always greater than our own earthly desires. Unlike us, God possesses a purely eternal perspective. He sees our lives from beginning to end. Despite our best human effort, His purely eternal perspective will always remain unmatched. We can and should fix our eyes on eternity, but we will never fully know how the tapestry of our lives will be woven together as a part of God's beautiful workmanship. Yet we have His Word, which provides us with knowledge of His goodness, promises of His love, and evidence of His mercy. Knowing and experiencing these aspects of God's character helps us to understand the promise of His purpose in our lives. Faith is central to such understanding. Hebrews 11:1 proclaims, "Faith is confidence in what we hope for and assurance about what we do not see." We can quote this verse or countless others regarding faith and the sovereignty of God daily. We can repeatedly verbalize our loss as "God's plan" and proclaim His love and goodness all day long. Still, if such actions are nothing more than words spewed forth to create the image of a strong Christian façade, then the truths that lie within these statements are rendered meaningless. Instead of *talking* about His plan and purpose, His goodness and love, we must allow these truths to penetrate the deep crevices of our very hearts, and *live* as though we believe it.

pause to journal . . .

- ☙ When reflecting upon God's purpose, goodness, and love, what does it look like to "live as though we believe it"?
- ☙ Are you living as though you believe it? How?

God's Will . . . for Will

I was so incredibly touched by one woman's explanation of the name she and her husband chose for their son, after giving birth to him at eighteen weeks. In Lindsey's Hope Story (appendix B), she shares, "We decided to name him Will since it was God's will that he not be born [to live on earth], but live forever in heaven with Jesus." This simple, yet profound statement conveys an attitude of trust in God's plan for her son's life. I can imagine that the very nature of their humanness was consumed by grief. Still, even in the midst of the grief, they were able to see God in the circumstances and believe that He had a plan for their son, Will. And what an amazing plan at that: to "live forever in heaven with Jesus." Simply precious.

God's will, though sometimes hard to discern or readily comprehend, is rooted and established in love. First Thessalonians 5:16–19 tells us clearly about the will of God for our lives in these words, "Rejoice always, pray continually, give thanks in all circumstances; for this is God's will for you in Christ Jesus." You may be thinking, *did He really mean* all *circumstances?* His Word is true and clearly asserts that His will for us in Christ is to rejoice, pray, and give thanks in *all* circumstances . . . even in times of loss. Those of us who have accepted the ultimate promise of Christ and are found in Him are able to do so with joy amidst our sorrow, recognizing the truth from Romans 8:28 that we talked about in chapter 3. Romans 8:28 confidently asserts, "And we know that in all things God works for the good of those who love him, who have been called according to his purpose." First off, *do you love Him?* God is calling you to a relationship with Him through His Son. He has called. He stands at the door and He knocks (Rev. 3:20). May you open the door of your heart to Him, receive His love, love Him in return, and live out the calling He has for your life—a life identified by who you are in Him, not only by the circumstances that brought you to Him.

hope for today ————————————————————

Now I want you to know, brothers and sisters, that what has happened to me has actually served to advance the gospel.

PHILIPPIANS 1:12

Purpose in the Pain

It's no easy task to find meaning in the midst of loss; purpose in the path of pain. When I think of this very concept, my mind goes to another Lindsay, a dear and precious friend. God brought Lindsay and me together as friends because of our experiences of loss. Her firstborn son, Andrew Lindsay, went to be with Jesus at twenty-one weeks gestation, just over a year after Chloe had died. A mutual friend put us in touch with one another. Neither of us could've imagined that a simple meeting over coffee would have been the beginnings of a ministry born out of the legacies of our children, Chloe Marie and Andrew Lindsay. These two tiny babies changed everything about who we were as women, as mothers, and as followers of Christ. By the end of our coffee date, we both knew that God had a purpose in our meeting that extended far beyond lending a listening ear to one another or extending comfort. We knew that He intended for us to use our experiences to reach out in His name. So began Mommies with Hope, a ministry neither of us would have ever chosen for ourselves, but was a direct result of our experiences.

When this all began, I don't think either of us fathomed that we would experience loss again. In fact, I became pregnant with a healthy baby shortly after the ministry officially began. I must admit, those initial weeks and months of the pregnancy were some of the most worrisome days. Everything seemed so tentative during that pregnancy. By God's will, I did give birth to a healthy baby girl. I was blessed. Just a few short months later Lindsay bore a healthy baby boy. All the world

61

seemed right. We had experienced our trial and had overcome. We were on the other side of things, ministering to others and fulfilling our calling in life. Nothing could go wrong; not again.

Sadly, this was not the end of either of our stories. In 2009, I experienced two miscarriages; one in my first trimester and one in my second trimester. After that, Lindsay too experienced a first-trimester miscarriage. I remember her telling me the news of her pregnancy; she was sick and tired, but oh so excited! A few short days later, I received this brief message in an email from her:

> I have very sad news—I am miscarrying our baby right now. Thank you for praying for me and our family. My only prayer is that God works a great miracle through this loss and His kingdom would be advanced.

Purpose in the pain. Literally, in the midst of her miscarriage, Lindsay was viewing the world with eyes fixed on eternity. Her simple prayer was filled with a hope for God's kingdom, that it may be advanced by others coming to know His Son, Jesus, as Savior. Like Paul, her words exuded a desire to advance the gospel. She believed in God's miraculous ability, yet trusted in His Sovereign plan. To me, Lindsay is a living testimony of one who possesses the ability to view purpose in the pain, a concept from which each of us can learn and grow.

pause to journal . . .

೬◆ Are you at a place where you can see purpose in the pain of your own loss? If yes, give examples. If no, first write your feelings about this answer. Then, pen a prayer asking God to show you purpose.

My Prayer for You, Fellow Mommy . . .

Lord, thank You for being the God with a plan and purpose for my life and the lives of each and every woman touched by miscarriage or infant loss, including this woman who reads this now. I admit that I don't always understand Your ways. I admit that I have questioned Your plans for me and for the other precious women with whom I've walked this long and difficult road. Lord, I pray that You help this woman to learn to trust in You. I pray, God, that You would reveal Your purposes to her in Your perfect timing. Help her to be patient, Lord. Give her eyes to see purpose in the pain, just as you did my friend Lindsay. Help this fellow mommy to find meaning through her precious baby's life, however brief it may have been. I trust You to help her find purpose in the pain. Amen.

Live It!

It can be difficult to see purpose in the midst of loss. Today, choose to be purposeful in carrying on the legacy of your child. Here are some ideas for how you can live life with purpose in the shadow of your loss:

- Donate to a child-related charity or organization in your baby's memory.

- Reach out to a fellow mommy who could use some encouragement. Send her a card, take her a meal, or invite her out for coffee.

- Write a letter to your baby, detailing the meaning or purpose you have discovered as a result of your child's brief life.

Write in your Hope Journal about what you did in honor of your baby.

verses to live by ————————————————

Many are the plans in a person's heart, but it is the LORD's purpose that prevails.

PROVERBS 19:21

◦◦◦

In their hearts humans plan their course, but the LORD establishes their steps.

PROVERBS 16:9

The Promise of Comfort

Blessed are those who mourn, for they will be comforted.

MATTHEW 5:4

Blessed are those who mourn? I'll be the first to admit that the Bible contains some perplexing statements. Are those who mourn really, truly blessed? This seems to be a bit of an oxymoron of sorts. Yet God is faithful and His Word is true, filled with promises for each one of us. The blessing for the mourner lies solely in the very truth that God provides the comfort. I can certainly recall times of blessing in the shadow of my own losses. There were women who brought meals for our family, friends who wrote encouraging notes, family who chose to acknowledge the painful reality of these members who would never physically be with us. I'm sure that you can think of examples of blessing in your own life too.

In all honesty, though, we're more likely to recall instances where others' action or inaction caused us pain. I vividly remember the pain I felt when certain family members and friends were absent from Chloe's funeral and visitation; family and friends whom I *expected* to see. The hurt surrounding this experience overshadowed the blessing of all who *were* present. There are countless other scenarios that come to mind where I wallowed in the hurt and disappointment of my grief and failed to recognize comfort in the midst of pain. Thus is the reality of living in a world where circumstances and people continuously fall short of our expectations and needs.

pause to journal . . .

→ Identify the people who have been a source of support in the shadow of your loss. How have you felt comforted by those people?

→ Are there times when you felt comfort was lacking? If so . . .
What expectations went unmet?
How did you cope with such disappointment?

God of All Comfort

What we truly need can only be fulfilled by one reliable source—our God who comforts. The apostle Paul starts out his second letter to the Corinthians giving praise to our God: "Praise be to the God and Father of our Lord Jesus Christ, the Father of compassion and the God of all comfort" (2 Cor. 1:3). This verse provides us with a wealth of insight about who God is. He is praiseworthy. He is not just compassionate; He is the Father of compassion. He is not just comforting; He is the God of *all* comfort. There's so much encouragement to glean from this small portion of Scripture.

God's promise of comfort does not look like the world's. It is not wrapped up in a treatment plan, found in a medicine bottle, or packaged nicely in a twelve-step program. The promise of His comfort, rather, stems from knowing Him; *really* knowing Him. In knowing, believing, and subsequently receiving the unfailing love of the Father (Ps. 119:76), demonstrated by the sacrificial love displayed on the cross of Christ (John 15:12–13), we can embrace His comfort in our own lives. In a beautiful analogy that resonates in our hearts, God says, "As a mother comforts her child, so will I comfort you" (Isa. 66:13). Knowing the Father through the Son enables the mourner to be blessed, the sorrowful to rejoice, and the griever to be glad—not because of the circumstances of life, but because of the truth that God is our comfort through the storm. Receiving such comfort, then, allows the comforted to become the comforter, used by God for His purpose and His glory.

pause to journal . . .

&> After reading 2 Corinthians 1:3–11, which verse(s) brings you the greatest comfort? Explain.

&> What did you learn about God's comforting character?

Real Comfort

God often uses other people to bring comfort to us, but it can be hard to genuinely accept comfort from others. Friends and loved ones have probably attempted to enter into your life and offer some sense of support. Many times, they leave the offer for comfort open-ended, suggesting that you "call if you need anything." Let's get real.

How likely are you to make that call? We may desperately need help, yet oftentimes our pride stands in the way of us reaching out to ask. Instead, we expect our loved ones to somehow read our minds and know just exactly what to do. After all, at least our husbands should know, right? If you haven't figured it out quite yet, either through your loss experience or in other areas of your marriage, husbands aren't mind readers either. Protectors? Yes. Providers? Yes. Companions, lovers, friends? Yes, yes, and yes. Your husband may be all of these things and more, and he may even be very insightful and sensitive to your feelings. I can guarantee, however, that he's no mind reader. We need to get real with ourselves and others, acknowledging that the unrealistic expectations we place on our loved ones—ahem, mind reading—only set us up for disappointment.

An area that I've personally struggled with in regard to this notion of real comfort is my need to be real with others. Often, we attempt to display a strong appearance of having it all together. Keeping up such a façade can be exhausting. Trust me, I know. The act is depleting. Trust me, I know. Behind closed doors, it is ugly. Trust me, I know.

I plead with an honest heart of full self-disclosure—allow others to enter into the messiness of your grief. In the days that followed the loss of Riyah Mae, my most recent loss, my sweet friend Lindsay very gently challenged me by saying, "Teske, there is a time to minister and a time to be ministered to. You need to let the body of Christ minister to you." I will never forget those words. Those words gave me *permission* to experience the blessing of others who had a desire and calling to comfort me in my grief. Those words were a genuine reality check and I was thankful. You see, Lindsay was doing only what God had called her to do as commanded in Galatians 6:2, "Carry each other's burdens, and in this way you will fulfill the law of Christ." Carry each other's burdens. We need to get real and we need to *be* real, so that we can position ourselves to experience real comfort, that the burden may be lightened. Receiving the promise of God's comfort means letting down the walls to allow Him and others to wrap us in their arms and provide the comfort that we so desperately need.

pause to journal . . .

&❧ How can you let God and others provide you with real comfort in the shadow of loss?

&❧ In what ways do you need to "get real" as you reflect upon receiving comfort?

hope for today ⎯⎯⎯⎯⎯⎯⎯⎯⎯⎯⎯⎯⎯

Praise be to the God and Father of our Lord Jesus Christ, the Father of compassion and the God of all comfort, who comforts us in all our troubles, so that we can comfort those in any trouble with the comfort we ourselves receive from God.

2 CORINTHIANS 1:3–4

Comfort Overflowing

There's just something about being with others who have "been there." When I learn of another woman who has experienced the loss of a baby, my heart genuinely hurts for her in the most tender way, yet I find comfort in our shared experience. I remember when I first met my ministry partner and friend, Lindsay. We met at a coffee shop, two individuals with a similar story, a broken heart, and a ludicrous love for the Savior. Independent of one another, we each felt a stirring in our hearts to reach out to other women who've been there. Women like us; women who love Jesus, long for Jesus, and need Jesus. During our time together, Lindsay shared with me the passage I mentioned above, 2 Corinthians 1:3–4:

> Praise be to the God and Father of our Lord Jesus Christ, the Father of compassion and the God of all comfort, who comforts us in all our troubles, so that we can comfort those in any trouble with the comfort we ourselves receive from God.

God brought us together for that very specific purpose: to comfort others who had "been there" with the comfort we have received from God. By the end of our time together, we had a support group meeting to plan. After all, Lindsay had already designed a logo and developed the name, Mommies with Hope, so it was a done deal; we were starting a support group.

pause to journal . . .

&~ Have you seen God use your experience of loss to enable you to comfort someone else?

hope for today ——————————————

And our hope for you is firm, because we know that just as you share in our sufferings, so also you share in our comfort.

2 CORINTHIANS 1:7

Sharing Comfort

In the handful of years since Chloe died, I've come to know many women who've gone through a similar experience; some who I was able to minister to for a season, others who have become the dearest of friends, and others still who I have walked alongside as their precious babies went to be with Jesus. It hurts to know that others have had to bear such a burden. It pains me to think about the fact that you are reading this book because you too have experienced the loss of a baby. Yet God has birthed true ministry out of the trials we face, the lessons we learn, and the comfort we receive from Him. As mommies who have been there, we share in the similarities of our grief experiences and, therefore, are able to share comfort. I pray this verse of encouragement over each of you now, which reads, "And our hope for you is firm, because we know that just as you share in our sufferings, so also you share in our comfort" (2 Cor. 1:7). Fellow mommy, my hope for you is firm.

Recently, I had the amazing honor and privilege of coming alongside a woman as she endured the loss of her precious son. Shayla had become a treasured friend through her involvement in the Mommies with Hope support groups. I had come to know Shayla after she had

experienced two previous losses. Understandably, Shayla was appre-
hensive about her new pregnancy, given her history. Each week went
by and our interactions had become a ritual of sorts. I would pray for
her at the start of each new week, knowing her appointment always
landed on Monday mornings. The subtle sound of my phone would
draw my attention to the awaited text: "There's a heartbeat!" "Heart
still beating." "Heartbeat is good." Week after week, the news was
good. Her little one was growing. Every so often, we would meet for
lunch after one of those Monday morning doctor appointments. More
often, though, she'd pick me up on Fridays and off we'd go into the
hustle and bustle of downtown for lunch. Talk of the baby would
surely ensue, prayers lifted up, and sometimes, a tentative excitement
would gleam through her eyes. That was our ritual week after week
throughout the summer.

A couple of Fridays ago, Shayla and I had lunch downtown again.
As we walked into the restaurant, we crossed paths with a pregnant
woman who we thought must have been full term. She was petite and
her baby belly resembled that of a basketball tucked under a fitted tur-
quoise cami that matched the rest of her professional attire perfectly.
I remember telling Shayla, "That's going to be you before long." We
laughed it off, acknowledging that our God-given bodies could never
look that way during pregnancy. We had a good talk that day, about
life, about loss, about the Lord, and about ministering to our fellow
mommies.

Sunday night, I received this text: "Pray for me . . . the infamous
sixteen-week appointment tomorrow." It was a mile marker of an
appointment, as her previous losses had all occurred at sixteen weeks
or prior. So the ritual continued. I prayed. I believed. I trusted. Monday morning came, busy with school appointments and a late arrival to
work. As expected, I soon heard the subtle sound of my text alert. This
time, "No heartbeat." Instinctively, I cried, "Oh no," sat at the table
in my office, buried my hands in my face as tears streamed down my
cheeks. Disbelief. I couldn't imagine what she was thinking, feeling,

experiencing in that moment. I had been there, but I could never know exactly what she must have felt. I knew it hurt and I wished to take every bit of it away.

A few text exchanges later and a brief update to my colleagues and I was headed over to the doctor's office. Sitting in that waiting room brought me back. I remember the first time I set foot in that office. It was here that we received news of Chloe's diagnosis. It was here we sat for many more visits to follow as we prepared for the death of our precious girl. It was here that we waited for visits during our pregnancy with our second daughter, Aiyana, a healthy girl who is now three. It was here we visited after spotting and bleeding in a subsequent pregnancy to learn that we were miscarrying at six weeks along. It was here where I entered that ultrasound room yet again . . . with joys and sorrows harbored deep within my soul, only to hear those very words myself—"No heartbeat"—as Riyah Mae had gone to be with Jesus at the beginning of my second trimester. Now, a dear friend, a sister in Christ, lay just beyond these fragile walls with the same news. News she'd heard before. News that no mother should ever have to hear. I wanted to be there, yet I didn't. I didn't want her to have to go through this *again*. I wanted to read the texts I had read before: "Heart still beating." Yet here I waited to be called back to join her and her husband in their mourning. All I could do was love her. Eventually, I was led to their ultrasound room. I know she's not a hugger, but I had resolved to hug her anyway. Hugs. Tears. Pain.

In this oh so familiar clinic, bittersweet with memories good and bad, we gathered our things and ourselves and we left out the back door—out of sight from the other parents in the waiting room with their bulging bellies. Our steps led us down the hallway, and just outside the elevator we greeted a mother with her four children, one babe still in his infant carrier. We took the stairs. As we left the clinic that day, we embarked on a week that was filled with tears, wrought with pain, yet wrapped in God's comfort. I couldn't take this pain from her, nor was there anything I could say or do to change the situation or bring her precious child back. I was simply there, sharing comfort.

One week later, she was doing the same. At the graveside memorial service for her own son, precious baby Tate, Shayla gave her fellow mommies a chance to honor their own children who were gone too soon. An array of flowers set the stage for a ceremony that I imagine is forever ingrained in the hearts and minds of those present. Family walked forward and laid flowers as they remembered: red roses from Tate's mommy and daddy, white roses from his big brother and sister, yellow roses in remembrance of his baby siblings who greeted him at heaven's gate, and blue carnations from close family members who honored his life. White carnations for all the mommies present who wished to honor their own children who had already gone to be with Jesus. One by one, mommy after mommy walked forward and retrieved a delicate white carnation to rest next to baby Tate. We were there for Tate—for Shayla and Joshua—yet they were there for us. In the darkest of times, they shined the beautiful light of Jesus as they lived in the promise of His comfort.

My Prayer for You, Fellow Mommy . . .

Dearest God of all comfort, be with us now. Help us to draw near to You and trust in You to provide us with comfort during our time of need. I pray that You would bring others into the life of this woman who can reach out to her and be a source of comfort. Lord, help her to know when to ask for help and to have the strength and courage to be willing to reach out to those who You place in her path to minister to her. I trust You will provide Your comfort to this woman. I ask, Lord Jesus, that in Your perfect timing and will that You would one day use her to be a comfort to someone else. In Your precious name, I pray. Amen.

Live It!

Examine yourself and consider whether you are in need of receiving comfort or at a place where you can genuinely give comfort. It's possible that you may feel a need and desire for both. Based on your conclusion, do one or both of the following:

- Express your need for comfort to your spouse or a trusted friend. Be clear in telling them how you are feeling at this point in your grief journey and asking them to help you in a way that would be meaningful for you.
- Think about how you can choose to be of comfort to someone else today. If you know someone who has experienced the loss of a baby, reach out to that person with a handwritten card or phone call. Gift that person with some sort of memento or token of remembrance as you honor their baby who died. Let them know that you are available to listen and pray with and for them.

verses to live by ————————————————

Just as you share in our sufferings, so also you share in our comfort.

2 CORINTHIANS 1:7

Carry each other's burdens, and in this way you will fulfill the law of Christ.

GALATIANS 6:2

The Promise of Peace

hope for today

Peace I leave with you; my peace I give you. I do not give to you as the world gives. Do not let your hearts be troubled and do not be afraid.

JOHN 14:27

Scripture reassures us that when we are crushed, broken, and torn with grief, the Lord is close by and He saves. He takes those broken bits and pieces and ever so gently mends us back together, binds us with His love, and envelops us in His peace. Sometimes, however, the grief is so great that we lose sight of Him and find ourselves simply broken.

Broken to Pieces

I recently attended a professional conference focusing on standards of care in hospital settings for families experiencing miscarriage or infant loss. I was struck by one of the presenter's stories. As a psychologist who specializes in women's reproductive psychology, the presenter had a great deal of experience in working with women who had endured miscarriage and infant loss, not to mention her own experience of giving birth to her daughter who was stillborn at nearly full term. Throughout the presentation, she recalled a variety of women's stories with whom she had worked over the years, as they related to the content of her teaching. One particular story caught my attention, the story of a mother who'd given birth to her stillborn baby boy who was nearly full term. There was no explanation for his death, as is often the case. She was so incredibly angry at the situation, understandably. During the pregnancy, this mother had prepared a nursery for her precious boy and was looking forward to bringing her healthy babe home to his room. Now, there would be no healthy baby to fill the crib, swaddle on the dressing table, or rock in the chair. Empty. Empty crib. Empty arms. Empty heart. That mom went home to a nursery filled with things—toys, décor, furniture, and a crib—all of which represented what should have been. In her grief, she destroyed the crib, smashing it to pieces. Broken pieces. Pieces that jutted, darted, and spiked out in all the wrong directions—just like the pieces of her broken heart. For a moment, she felt better. Still, she was broken, just like the crib that was meant to cradle her sleeping boy.

pause to journal . . .

- ﹋ Can you relate to the story above? Have you reacted in a similar way in your brokenness?
- ﹋ What has your brokenness looked like in the shadow of your loss?
- ﹋ How have you coped with your brokenness?

hope for today

The LORD is close to the brokenhearted and saves those who are crushed in spirit.

PSALM 34:18

Lord, Piece [Peace] Me Together

In the midst of my brokenness, I would cry out, "Lord, piece me together!" I remember those hard nights all too well; nights when I would lie in bed until my husband fell asleep so that I could cry in secret. I cried hard and despite my efforts to muffle the tears, my shaking body often woke Justin from his slumber. Half sleeping, he would hold me as I cried. All I could muster to say amidst the tears is, "It's not fair! I just want her here. I just want her here, that's all!" I would repeat these words over and over, night after night. I felt incomplete, as though something was missing. In some ways, I was asking God to give Chloe back, and if only He did this one thing, all would be well. Oh yes, I bargained! I learned that God isn't the bargaining type. He doesn't have to be because He already has a perfect plan in place. I had to get to a place of peace, where even in her absence, all was well. I needed Him to piece me together with His peace.

As time went on, I realized more and more just how much I needed Him to piece me together. I began to identify triggers in my life that brought about a mess of feelings and emotions. Simply seeing a pregnant woman in the grocery store could generate feelings of envy. Envy gave root to tinges of bitterness as I allowed the "I want what she's got" mentality to settle in. Anger would come easily—again, at the store—when I witnessed mothers yelling, threatening, or mistreating their children. I would think to myself, "How dare her! She should be so grateful." We face these situations daily, and when accompanied by messy, broken grief, we are left vulnerable. It's much easier to fall into the trap of being consumed by our emotions in a state of discontent than it is to rest in God's purpose and peace. What is easy, however, is not always wise.

A fellow mommy eloquently expressed to me that when she experienced miscarriage, she felt as though she was robbed of the joy of pregnancy. It was no longer "innocent," as she referred to it. Instead, anxiety and uncertainty filled her thoughts and consumed her heart as she and her husband considered trying again. Perhaps you can relate, as you have either experienced or contemplated subsequent pregnancy. In healthy pregnancy after loss, many women wrestle with striking a balance with their emotions. They long to celebrate the healthy baby that now grows within, but they are plagued with feelings of guilt and anxiety, juggling between the joy over the baby expected to arrive and the grief over the baby who died. Subsequent pregnancy is often viewed in a tentative fashion. Tentative, because we have learned that a healthy baby is not a guarantee. Fear and anxiety wash over and sometimes threaten to consume our hearts. Our human inclination is to become wrapped up in our circumstances, rather than our Savior. We must become more. What we need is peace. Peace in the depth of our souls about the loss, peace as we adjust to our new normal, and peace for the plans that He has in store.

hope for today

Let the peace of Christ rule in your hearts.

COLOSSIANS 3:15

pause to journal . . .

- In the shadow of your loss, what areas in your life are in opposition to living the promise of God's peace?
- How do you combat such discord?
- What are some new tools or strategies that you could implement that will allow the peace of Christ to rule your heart?

hope for today

You will keep in perfect peace those whose minds are steadfast, because they trust in you.

ISAIAH 26:3

Perfect Peace

Peace is not a description of our circumstances. Rather, it is a depiction of our hearts. It *is* possible to possess a heart of peace amidst circumstances that are seemingly out of control. Experiencing God's promise of peace starts first by having a relationship with Him. We have already uncovered several other promises of God that help us to understand how such a relationship is possible. We have learned about the promise of God's unfailing, unconditional, sacrificial love for each of us, demonstrated by the ultimate promise—Jesus. The verse above tells us that God gives those who trust in Him a sense of "perfect peace." We truly trust in God by believing in what His Son, Jesus, did on the cross. In John 14:6–7 Jesus explains, "I am the way and the truth and the life. No one comes to the Father except through me. If you really know me, you will know my Father as well." Plainly stated, we can't know the Father without knowing the Son! When we know the Son, we open our hearts up to experiencing God's abundant promises, including the promise of His peace. Trusting in Jesus brings a peace that transcends our earthly understanding (Phil. 4:7).

Possessing such a peace enables the impossible to occur in the midst of loss. I have seen many examples of such impossible peace in my own life and in the lives of women who've walked a similar path. It's only the peace of God that allowed . . .

A mommy to labor for her baby, already dead, and proclaim, "I really am blessed. I am so thankful."

A mommy to continue on with a pregnancy, honoring her unborn son's life by beautifully documenting the activities and outings they took him on, knowing he was guaranteed to die.

A mommy to sit in a silent ultrasound room where no heartbeat was found and say, "God, I trust You."

A mommy to see purpose behind her son's brief life as she gives glory to God for all He has done.

I share these examples above for a specific purpose—to give glory to God and show how He has brought His peace into these real women's lives. I pray that you are encouraged by the examples above and that you do not let yourself dwell on how you should or should not have responded when facing a similar situation. In our own fleshly strength, we react to our circumstances based on feelings and emotions. These women relied on God's strength, realizing that apart from Him, they are inept. It was God, working in them, who brought peace amidst the pain. The peace of God makes the impossible, possible; and the unbearable, bearable. We *can* rejoice with peace in our hearts, not because of our losses or our circumstances. We rejoice because of who He is and how He has gifted us with His peace to make it through one more day.

hope for today —————————————————————

Rejoice in the Lord always. I will say it again: Rejoice! Let your gentleness be evident to all. The Lord is near. Do not be anxious about anything, but in every situation, by prayer and petition, with thanksgiving, present your requests to God. And the peace of God, which transcends all understanding, will guard your hearts and your minds in Christ Jesus.

PHILIPPIANS 4:4–7

—————————————————————————— *pause to journal . . .*

- ❧ Have you experienced moments of peace in the shadow of your loss? Explain.
- ❧ What obstacles do you feel are in the way of you personally experiencing the promise of God's peace?
- ❧ Based on the Scriptures shared above, how can you overcome such obstacles?

hope for today ——————————————————

But now in Christ Jesus you who once were far away have been brought near by the blood of Christ. For he himself is our peace.

EPHESIANS 2:13–14

Brought Near

The nearness of God can't be measured by the amount of time we spend in church or how many good deeds we do each day. God is near when we recognize our need for His mercy, acknowledge His Son as our Savior, and kneel at the foot of His throne. It's not about rites and rituals done in an attempt to reach God. It's all about a relationship with Him through His Son, Jesus Christ. As you may recall, God Himself tells us, "You will seek me and find me when you seek me with all your heart" (Jer. 29:13). He is simply waiting for us to draw near to Him. As clearly stated in Ephesians 2:13 above, we are brought near by Christ's blood. The finished work of Christ on the cross is what allows us to have a relationship with God and experience the promises He has in store for us, including the promise of His peace.

An interesting finding through studying God's peace is that it's often associated with the nearness of God. In the shadow of loss, you may feel as though God is far-off, distant, or blatantly oblivious. I recently heard a speaker share on the topic of grief at a secular work conference. In reference to a story he was sharing, depicting the unfair nature of a young person's death, he repeatedly questioned, "Why wasn't God watching?" This may be precisely the way you feel. In the midst of the questioning in this auditorium, I wanted to stand and proclaim with confidence, backed up by God's Word, "He was watching. He was there. He knew about it from the dawning of time. I can picture Him crying and grieving and hurting. He knows the pain of this grief. He is with us now. His plans are greater than you can fathom and He will work this out for good. He will draw others to Himself. I trust Him." Rather, I sat and I prayed and I thought all of these things, reminding myself that He is good, He is near, and He brings peace. And, I kept my job.

pause to journal . . .

&> Read the following Scripture passages. For each passage, consider the following question: What encouragement is offered regarding the nearness of God?
- Psalm 73:28
- Hebrews 10:22–23
- James 4:7–10

To understand how we've been "brought near" by the blood of Christ, it's important for us to grasp our stance with God before this sacrifice. Prior to Jesus' shedding of blood, we were cut off from God. Nothing could bridge the gap between man's sinfulness and God's holiness. In His divinity, God made a way through the cross where His Son, Jesus, gave His life. Romans 3:25 reiterates this point in stating, "God presented Christ as a sacrifice of atonement, through the shedding of his blood—to be received by faith. He did this to demonstrate his righteousness, because in his forbearance he had left the sins committed beforehand unpunished." It is through our faith in this shedding of Jesus' blood that we are reconciled to a right relationship with God in Christ. It is His shed blood that saves us and brings us peace—peace with God and peace in our hearts. Jesus died on the cross and was beaten, bruised, and crushed for us so that in our brokenness, He may be our peace and piece us back together.

My Prayer for You, Fellow Mommy . . .

Heavenly Father, send us Your peace. Lord, I pray that You wrap this woman with a blanket of peace that only You can provide, shielding her from the anxieties, fears, turmoil, and confusion that may surface. Lord, take the brokenness of this mommy's heart and piece it back together with a peace that comes from You alone. Help her to know, sense, and experience Your nearness to her, oh God. Make Yourself known to this woman in an intimate, personal, and real way so that she may experience a peace that surpasses any human understanding. Amen.

Live It!
Take some time to get away, if possible. Create a peaceful setting for yourself—your favorite coffee shop, an outdoor space of retreat, or in the quietness of your home. Spend some time in prayer, asking God to bring you His peace. Write in your Hope Journal if you'd like.

verses to live by ⸻

You will keep in perfect peace those whose minds are steadfast, because they trust in you.

ISAIAH 26:3

❧ ☙

But now in Christ Jesus you who once were far away have been brought near by the blood of Christ. For he himself is our peace.

EPHESIANS 2:13–14

❧ ☙

Let the peace of Christ rule in your hearts.

COLOSSIANS 3:15

The Promise of Refinement

In all this you greatly rejoice, though now for a little while you may have had to suffer grief in all kinds of trials. These have come so that the proven genuineness of your faith—of greater worth than gold, which perishes even though refined by fire—may result in praise, glory and honor when Jesus Christ is revealed.

1 PETER 1:6–7

Refinement is a process used to remove impurities and unwanted elements from substances such as oil, gold, silver, and other precious metals, with the ultimate goal being purity and perfection. The process of refinement can also be examined from a spiritual perspective. Consider the verses above. The substance to which our faith is compared is that of gold. The natural disposition and appearance of gold is far from the images that come to mind when we picture this precious metal. It's not discovered in precisely formed bars or in strands of tiny chain links, waiting to be threaded with the perfect charm. In its natural state, gold is found in unsightly masses, some large, most tiny. To truly become something beautiful, the gold must go through a refining process, which provides us with the beautiful, finished, and complete result that comes to mind.

We too need to be refined. Our natural state is undesirable to say the least. We have already established that all are sinners (Rom. 3:23). This includes you, me, our children, our pastors, and every person on this earth. This is our sinful nature. The apostle Paul, a man who by God's inspiration penned a large portion of the New Testament and who refers to himself as the "worst of sinners" (1 Tim. 1:16), transparently shares his own struggle with sin:

> For I know that good itself does not dwell in me, that is, in my sinful nature. For I have the desire to do what is good, but I cannot carry it out. For I do not do the good I want to do, but the evil I do not want to do—this I keep on doing. (Rom. 7:18–19)

By the same token, there are those of us who may appear to have a refined appearance, yet are crumbling on the inside. Outside appearances may indicate that we've got it together and that life is a bed of roses. Outside appearances, however, can be quite deceiving. While such a façade may be attractive to people, God sees straight through the charade into the deep crevices of our very hearts and souls. If we're honest, what looks appealing on the outside is often appalling on the inside. He knows about the hidden grief that has been bottled in, and He sees the bitterness take root. Instead of trying to hide it, let *Him* be your hiding place. First Samuel 16:7 asserts, "The LORD does not look at the things people look at. People look at the outward appearance, but the LORD looks at the heart." He sees me. He sees you.

He already knows the mess that resides within, so why try to shield Him from what He already knows? Rather, pour it all out to Him. Lay it at His feet and in the words of David's psalm, cry out, "Create in me a pure heart, O God, and renew a steadfast spirit within me" (Ps.

51:10). He is ever so faithful to answer the cries of our hearts when we humbly bow before Him. Allow the sufferings and trials, the pain of your grief, to serve as a refining fire. This refining fire, by God's grace alone, will shape and mold each of us into the woman He has created us to be. We are precious in His sight. Won't you welcome Him in, to walk alongside you in your grief?

hope for today

Create in me a pure heart, O God, and renew a steadfast spirit within me.

PSALM 51:10

pause to journal . . .

- ❧ Are there areas in your life that you need to let God in to do His refining work? If yes, make note of these areas.
- ❧ Have you experienced God's refining work in your grief journey? Explain what He has taught you.

hope for today

I consider that our present sufferings are not worth comparing with the glory that will be revealed in us.

ROMANS 8:18

For a Little While

Enduring the days of mourning is hard work. It is my prayer that you get to a place of letting God transform your perspective. The Hope for Today verse above, Romans 8:18, gives us a glimpse of hope as we consider future glory. For now, in the immediate aftermath of your loss experience, you may feel numb and lack any sense of time. Your days are a jumbled mess and you feel frozen in your footsteps. This haze of grief can last a long while, and once overcome, may only seem to be a blur. It can be especially difficult as you begin to move out of the fog of grief and begin to rejoin reality, where everyone else has continued to move along quite well in your mental and physical absence. I say this facetiously, yet with a true sense of compassionate understanding for those of you who've had this experience. For the newly bereaved, consider this an advance warning. The days and months after Chloe died seem like a complete blur to me. I recall coming out of this haze in the fall, just in time for the holidays.

With a true type-A, control freak personality (I confess), I did everything I could to prepare myself for the holidays. We attended a grief symposium on the topic and I purposed to "do something" in her memory. We *did* many things. It's fabulous to have a plan and I encourage preparation. I truly believe it helped. What I wasn't prepared for, however, was the holiday I hadn't even considered would be a problem. It was this holiday—the one complete with worthy goals and resolutions—that brought me the most grief. Happy New Year! Unlikely. In a *Mommies with Hope* blog post, written in light of the new year, I wrote about the struggle that this time of year brings, but more importantly the significance of keeping our eyes fixed on eternity:

If you've known me for a while, then you probably know that I've often remarked about how New Year's tends to be a difficult time of the year for me, personally. In fact, I recall the first year of holidays after Chloe's birth and death and was shocked by the impact of New Year's. After all, it's a time for new beginnings and resolutions. For a grieving mommy, however, it can be a reminder that time and people are moving on, yet she continues to long for her baby.

This year marks the fifth New Year since Chloe's birth and death. The first two years were the most difficult, with the second year being the worst. Last year wasn't the greatest either, in light of my miscarriages of Jesse and Riyah in 2009. Yet, with each passing year, I am able to sense God's peace and purpose through each of my babies' lives. Several months ago, a dear and precious friend gently reminded me that on earth, it would literally be impossible to have all of my children since some of the pregnancies overlapped. However, I can rest in the knowledge that God, who is rich in mercy, has welcomed each one of my babies into His kingdom already! Because my husband and I know Christ as our Savior, we have *full assurance* in reuniting with each of them when He calls us home. Lord willing, our two living children will come to know Jesus at the earliest possible age, and they too will be with us all for eternity! What a family reunion that will be!

Especially in difficult times, I have learned the significance of having an eternal perspective. That being said, it can be tough when the grief is so raw and the pain is so real. So if you're like me, you may just be wondering how to face the day.

"Because of the LORD's great love we are not consumed,
  for his compassions never fail.
They are new every morning;
  great is your faithfulness." (Lam. 3:22–23)

I love these verses from Lamentations 3! At times, grief may seem to be all-consuming. God's love is greater. Because of such great love, we are not consumed! He has *compassion* for each one of us, whom He loves. Other translations use the word *mercies* in place of *compassions* . . . each of which are new every morning. Every day when we wake up, the Lord is near. He loves us. He never fails us. He is faithful. He wants to bless us each and every day with His mercies. Though we know this to be true from Scripture, it can be hard to feel this way. *That's why it's important to rely on what is true, rather than our feelings.* The next verse in this passage goes on to say, "The LORD is my portion" (v. 24). Here are some questions to ponder in light of this verse: Is He your portion each and every day? Do you rise each morning with the knowledge of God's love and compassion for you? Is He enough? The biblical truth shared above may seem to be "good for the moment" but how can you live like you know it to be true? How can you live victoriously, proclaiming, "The LORD is my portion"? What does that even look like?

pause to journal . . .

» Read and reflect upon the questions posed at the end of the blog post shared above. Write your thoughts in your Hope Journal now.

Through the difficult experience of witnessing others move on, while I felt so completely stuck, I learned a valuable lesson. Grief has no timeline and that's okay. If I keep my eyes fixed on eternity, there's a hope that wells up within me and brings me peace to make it through each day. I trust that God has wonderful things in store, in this life and certainly in the next. I pray you'll join me as you allow God to refine your perspective—from enduring this existence to envisioning eternity.

hope for today ———————————————

So we fix our eyes not on what is seen, but on what is unseen, since what is seen is temporary, but what is unseen is eternal.

2 CORINTHIANS 4:18

Surrender

Allowing God to refine our hearts means that we first have to humble ourselves to let Him in. I have a treasured friend and fellow mommy who exemplifies such a refining surrender. Amanda and her husband, Craig, have come to be special friends over the years. We met through our church after both being invited to another member's home for lunch one Sunday after services. At that time, Amanda was newly pregnant with her first child. Just a few weeks after our lunch gathering, Amanda had her first ultrasound at around twenty weeks along. I had not kept in touch with Amanda outside of church or gotten to know her any further from our initial lunch together, but I vividly recall the day that changed everything about our friendship.

My husband and I were sitting in our friend's dining room one evening, spending some time in fellowship and in the Word. Jen and Doug also attended our church and were close friends with the pastor, whose phone call to Doug interrupted our conversation. I could tell by Doug's tone and demeanor that the news was not good. After a brief phone conversation, Doug told the rest of us that Pastor Dave had called to request prayer for our fellow church members, Craig and Amanda, and their unborn son. The ultrasound indicated that their baby had a condition that was incompatible with life: anencephaly—an absence of the brain and skull. I knew all about this. I was, after all, the teaching assistant for an infant development and guidance course at the time. A little over one year prior, we had faced our own diagnosis experience with Chloe. Before Doug had even uttered all that Pastor Dave had told him, I knew what this meant for them. Tears filled my eyes and sympathy welled up deep within my soul as I recalled all too well the pain of the reality they now faced.

Noah was born full term on August 20, 2007, and lived for three days—longer than anyone expected. He was so strong. Over the course of those twenty weeks between the time of Noah's diagnosis and his birth, my husband and I came to know Craig and Amanda as they invited us into their lives to walk this journey with them. I could literally write an entire book on all that their friendship and Noah's life taught us. For now, however, I want to focus on the amazing testimony exhibited through their lives, especially as it relates to a surrendering that occurred years later. While they surrendered to God's will with Noah's diagnosis, his brief life, and anticipated death, and praised God through the storm of grief, the difficulties were unrelenting in the years that followed Noah's death.

Grief gave way to longing (and trying) for another baby. What seemed to come so easily with Noah was now a challenge. They found themselves in the midst of a different kind of grief—a grief that some of you may be able to relate to—the grief of fertility struggles. Month after month would go by and hope for a child would continue to build, only for those dreams to be dashed. They sought the help of fertility specialists in their efforts to conceive. Becoming pregnant began to consume Amanda and she learned some valuable lessons and grew in her relationship with God through the struggles that followed Noah's birth and death. One late spring evening, Amanda sent me the following brief message in an email, "I don't know why I am sending this tonight, but here it is." Attached was a journal entry of sorts, reflecting on the hard lesson in surrender God was teaching her. Though she did not know at the time *why* she was sending it, we now know that it was meant to be shared. I pray you are blessed, encouraged, challenged, and refined as you read her words below.

The desire to have children is a Godly desire, His Word tells us to be fruitful and multiply. However, for my husband and me it has not been that easy. Our first son died shortly after birth and now we have tried for two years to get pregnant. At the end of January we did get pregnant and, shortly after we found out we were expecting, we miscarried.

I have wanted nothing more than having children and this is a problem for me. My desire for children has become the focus and the all-consuming presence in my life. Until a couple of months ago I didn't see this as a problem and the desire is not the problem; the fact that it has taken first place in my life is the problem.

The Holy Spirit has been at work in my heart and convicting

me that my priorities are wrong. My plans for tonight did not include reading for the group study I have tomorrow (because I wasn't planning on going). However, the Spirit is more powerful than my plans and led me to pick up that book. In the chapter for tomorrow the author, Elyse Fitzpatrick (*Idols of the Heart: Learning to Long for God Alone*), asked the questions:

"Does this desire fulfill God's design?" *Yes, children most certainly do!*
"Does Jesus occupy the first place in this desire?" *Well . . .*
"Is He my God or have I made a god of this longing?" *Ouch!*

I have made this longing first priority in my life for far too long. Fitzpatrick pointed me to the stories of Rachel and Hannah. Rachel's desire had become a sin because it took God's place in her heart. Hannah's desire was not sin because she desired God first and children to enhance her relationship with God.

I'd like to say that I'm in between these ladies but there is not a sin scale, sin is sin. Plain and simple I have been putting getting pregnant before God, which, let's face the facts, I'm not getting pregnant without Him. Revelation 4:11 tells me, "For you created all things, and by your will they were created and have their being." If I am having a child, it's only by his will. So, shouldn't He be first in my life?

Now let me be honest here, just because I have made the realization doesn't mean that it's easy for me to fix. I have to strive to put God first, my husband second, and getting pregnant somewhere after that (currently I'm not even sure it should be third). I must strive to be like Hannah, seeking joy in God, turning to prayer, and putting my desires in His will.

In God's sovereignty, Amanda sent me this message at a time that to the world may seem to be pure irony. Unbeknownst to her, she was actually pregnant. They conceived after they *stopped* fertility treatments. It was also fresh off the heels of our church's women's retreat—a bittersweet weekend filled with pregnant women, newborn babies, nursing moms, and motherhood, all of which seemed to be a slap in the face. Though Satan tried to get the best of her, God's victory prevailed as He used that weekend to bring her to a point of broken, humble, genuine submission to His will. Together, with our pastor's wife, we cried and prayed and handed the hurt over to God in true surrender. Just a few months later, I was asked to share a devotion at Amanda's baby shower. There, we honored Noah and his baby sibling in heaven, cherished the miracle of God's mercy and creation, and marveled at all He had taught her by sharing her own words, as written above. She had walked through a refining fire and was able to come out on the other side surrendered and sanctified with a strength that came from the Savior.

For Amanda, surrender meant giving her desire for children over to God and leaving the results up to Him. In the shadow of miscarriage and infant loss, there are many areas where women may struggle. Perhaps you have tried to maintain control of your grief. If you are anything like I was, you may be grappling to hold it all together, conveying an attitude of strength and control, when on the inside you are truly falling apart. Others of you may be struggling with an immense anxiety about trying again, wondering whether you should and if so, how you can face another pregnancy. Is it time to relinquish control, surrender to God's refining process, and let Him do the healing work that only He can do?

pause to journal . . .

> Look within and assess whether there are any areas where you need to surrender and let God do His refining work in your life. Take some time to reflect on these areas now and write about them.

My Prayer for You, Fellow Mommy . . .

Lord, I bow before You, acknowledging that I don't understand all of Your ways. Still, I trust You and pray that You would continue to mold and refine me into the woman that You have created me to be. Father, I ask that You would make Yourself known to this very precious woman who is traveling a similar path, wrought with grief as she mourns the loss of her baby. Help her to surrender to Your refining work in her life, Lord. If there are areas that she needs to relinquish control of, I pray that she would hand those areas over to You in humble surrender. Continue to fashion each of us according to Your divine will. In Jesus' precious name, I pray. Amen.

Live It!

Today, spend some quiet time in prayer and ask God to reveal to you those areas where He can do His refining work. Consider these practical suggestions as you prayerfully surrender to God's refining work in your life:

- Purpose to wake up fifteen minutes earlier than usual each day. Begin your day in prayer, pouring your heart out to God. Remember, He has compassion for you!
- Saturate yourself in God's Word. When we feel consumed by our grief, His Word is our strength and gives us the ability to "take captive every thought to make it obedient to Christ" (2 Cor. 10:5). Consider memorizing some of the Hope for Today verses shared throughout this book.
- Thank God for the blessings in your life. Purpose to find something to be thankful for. Ask God to be your portion for the day . . . the hour . . . the moment. He is faithful!

verses to live by ————————————————

Let perseverance finish its work so that you may be mature and complete, not lacking anything.

JAMES 1:4

◦◦

I consider that our present sufferings are not worth comparing with the glory that will be revealed in us.

ROMANS 8:18

◦◦

For you, God, tested us; you refined us like silver.

PSALM 66:10

The Promise of Restoration

hope for today —————————————

And the God of all grace, who called you to his eternal glory in Christ, after you have suffered a little while, will himself restore you and make you strong, firm and steadfast.

1 PETER 5:10

Having experienced loss, we are forever changed. In this world, we will never be the same. Our children's lives, no matter how brief, mattered. They meant something. We will never be the women we were before we became pregnant with the little ones for whom we now grieve. We will *always* be those precious babies' mommies. In their absence, there's an emptiness that prevails. The emptiness manifests itself in various forms, including physical, emotional, and perhaps spiritual emptiness. The pages to come will explore each of these forms and the truth from God's Word about His promise of restoration.

Physical

A longing in your arms and a vacancy in your body are the markers of the physical emptiness you may be feeling. Such physical emptiness is especially prevalent in the early days after loss. For those of us who've experienced miscarriage, we face the fact that our once firm or bulging bellies are no longer occupied by the life that grew within. For all of us, there's an aching in our arms as we long to cradle our babies. There's also a physical emptiness that accompanies the physiological effect of milk production after loss. The discomfort serves as yet another reminder of the fact that there's no living baby to nourish or care for. Our bodies change, bleeding ensues, and pain remains. Yet Jesus Himself says, "Come to me, all you who are weary and burdened, and I will give you rest" (Matt. 11:28). He invites us to come. He longs to ease our pain and give us rest. Will you let Him?

Emotional

In the shadow of loss, we experience a range of emotions. Shock, numbness, sadness, devastation, confusion, guilt, and the list goes on. It's this range of emotions, all jumbled together, that paints the picture of our grief. When we think about our emotions in terms of an emotional emptiness, isolation comes to mind. Perhaps you can relate to this sense of feeling completely alone in your loss experience. Such loneliness may even exist as you struggle to make sense of how the loss of your baby has impacted your marriage. After all, your husband lost a child too, so shouldn't he understand completely? Shouldn't he know what you are feeling and know just how to respond? No, he shouldn't, because he is experiencing his personal grief in his own unique way. That is the nature of grief. It is individual to each person and no two people will grieve just alike, no matter what their experience or relationship. Only God truly understands. Scripture tells us, "God is our refuge and strength, an ever-present help in trouble" (Ps. 46:1). Psalm 34:17 assures us, "The righteous cry out, and the LORD hears them; he delivers them from all their troubles." Jesus Himself can "empathize with our weaknesses" (Heb. 4:15). Let us pour our hearts out to Him, our God who truly understands.

Spiritual

A spiritual emptiness, void, or turmoil may ensue after loss as you wrestle with the many tough questions about life and death, and how to factor God into the equation. Some seek out God as they strengthen, renew, and rely on their faith to see them through. Others reject God and question His ways, feeling betrayed or punished by a *supposedly* all-loving God. "Why?" questions linger, as attempts to understand a senseless death perpetuate the questioning. In times of questioning, I find great comfort in Ecclesiastes 11:5 which reads, "As you do not know the path of the wind, or how the body is formed in a mother's womb, so you cannot understand the work of God, the Maker of all things." We simply don't understand, not because God is secretive, sly, or out to get us with His hidden agenda. We cannot understand because His ways are too marvelous (Job 37:5) and no one can fathom His understanding (Isa. 40:28). Spiritual emptiness is an ominous place to reside, characterized by hopelessness. Such emptiness can only be filled by God. Psalm 16:11 gives encouragement and satisfies a longing soul by saying, "You make known to me the path of life; you will fill me with joy in your presence, with eternal pleasures at your right hand." When we let God fill our empty hearts with His presence, He equips us to face the physical and emotional emptiness in the shadow of our loss. God doesn't promise to shield us from the grief, but He will gladly walk through it with us if we invite Him on the journey.

pause to journal . . .

ε❧ In what ways have you felt emptiness in the shadow of your loss?
ε❧ How can you let God fill the emptiness?

hope for today ───────────────

Then He who sat on the throne said, "Behold, I make all things new."

REVELATION 21:5 NKJV

Miracles

God is in the miracle business. To the majority of you, this is probably not a completely startling revelation. You've heard the stories, right? Jesus fed thousands with two fish and five loaves of bread (John 6:1–15), He made the blind man see (9:1–12), He brought Lazarus back to life (11:38–43), and He overcame the grave Himself (20:1–29)! Even before His blessed dwelling among men, God was in the miracle business. Let's think of some Old Testament examples: the parting of the Red Sea (Exod. 14) or daily rain showers of manna in the desert for His chosen people (Exod. 16). Not to mention that He created the entire universe in a mere six days (Gen. 1).

God performs miracles, even now. You may read this statement and think: "Really? Miracles? Hmmm. Then why didn't God miraculously heal my baby? Why didn't He let him or her live? If God is truly in the 'miracle business,' then why am I left here to grieve?" These are tough questions. Questions I've heard many women voice, and questions that I've pondered myself. God makes miracles out of our messes. He willingly takes on the messiness of our grief and transforms it into a thing of beauty. The only condition is that we have to let Him. In the gospel of Luke, Jesus quotes Scripture from Isaiah. The Isaiah passage reads:

> The Spirit of the Sovereign LORD is on me,
> because the LORD has anointed me
> to proclaim good news to the poor.
> He has sent me to bind up the brokenhearted,
> to proclaim freedom for the captives

and release from darkness for the prisoners,
to proclaim the year of the LORD's favor. (61:1–2)

In Luke 4:21, Jesus declares, "Today this scripture is fulfilled in your hearing." In other words, He was declaring Himself, the promised Messiah, as the fulfillment of the Scriptures. In the original passage from the prophet Isaiah, the Scripture goes on to say,

[He has sent me] to comfort all who mourn,
  and provide for those who grieve in Zion—
to bestow on them a crown of beauty
  instead of ashes,
the oil of joy
  instead of mourning,
and a garment of praise
  instead of a spirit of despair.
They will be called oaks of righteousness,
  a planting of the LORD
  for the display of his splendor. (61:2–3)

The latter verses offer an amazing promise to us. Jesus is here to comfort, and in doing so, turn our grief and mourning into something beautiful—all for His glory. This is the restorative promise of our God! Today, I implore you to join me in choosing to see His miracles beyond the mess.

pause to journal . . .

- What comfort can you glean from the truth shared in the verses above (Isa. 61:1–3)?
- What miracle beyond the mess of your own loss experience can you choose to see?

By trusting in God's promises for our lives, we draw near to Him by faith. In the shadow of loss, we're left with a void. Nothing but Jesus can fill that empty space in our hearts. And when we let Him, there is healing on the horizon.

hope for today —————————————————————

Though you have made me see troubles, many and bitter, you will restore my life again; from the depths of the earth you will again bring me up. You will increase my honor and comfort me once more.

PSALM 71:20–21

Healing

In the summer of 2010, Grandma died after having just turned eighty-seven years old. She was special for many reasons, but one of the things that made her especially unique is that she birthed seventeen babies into this world. Three of her babies died during pregnancy, twins and another baby, all stillborn. Growing up, I had learned about my mother's baby siblings in heaven. However, it wasn't something that was talked about in depth. Even to her last days, Grandma remembered her precious babies. They were special to her. In the years leading up to Grandma's death, she became ill. In light of her ailing health, she planned much of her funeral ahead, with details recorded on loose leaf paper, penned by her own hand. In her handwritten obituary, she acknowledged loved ones who had preceded her in death, including her little ones. She acknowledged her great-grandchildren who had gone to be with Jesus too. In that moment, though Grandma was gone, I felt powerfully bonded to her through our shared experience of loss. Though we never talked about it together, she got it. She remembered her own, and mine too. I regret never asking her to tell me about her babies. I imagine it would have helped us both.

I find this important to point out for a couple of reasons. Like Grandma, we'll never forget our babies who are in heaven. They are forever a part of us, and we have the amazing opportunity to carry on their legacies and teach the generations to come about these members in our families who were gone too soon. In doing so, we are choosing to honor our babies' lives and make the point that their lives had weight in this world.

Also, we must remember that God's healing power is never out of reach, regardless of how old you are or how long it has been since your loss experience. At our very first Mommies with Hope support group meeting in the fall of 2007, we had a woman attend who miscarried her baby in 1988. She was apologetic as she shared her story, acknowledging that it had been almost twenty years. Still, she felt a desire to come and seek out support because she'd never had the opportunity to share this experience with others who'd been through something similar. We responded to this precious woman with love and shared the same truths from Scripture with her that we shared with all the other women in attendance who were grieving very recent losses. God's Word and His promises are timeless. When a woman enters into a new life in Christ (2 Cor. 5:17), true healing is possible. When she opens her heart to the restorative work He has in store for her, healing begins.

Psalm 71:20–21 conveys the promise of God's healing, restorative promises for our lives. These verses read, "Though you have made me see troubles, many and bitter, you will restore my life again; from the depths of the earth you will again bring me up. You will increase my honor and comfort me once more." The psalmist confidently proclaims, "You will restore my life again." There's no hesitation or doubt in this statement. He doesn't say *if* You restore my life. Rather, he asserts, You *will* restore my life again. The Bible is not filled with people's opinions; it is a gathering of God's promises! What a treasured gift to know that He will restore us, give us strength, and make us steadfast (1 Peter 5:10).

hope for today

I have told you these things, so that in me you may have peace. In this world you will have trouble. But take heart! I have overcome the world.

JOHN 16:33

Where healing and restoration meet, victory prevails. This meeting occurs at the cross.

In the flesh, we sense the sting of death. We feel the pain, the hurt, the emptiness, and the grief. God created us to feel; we're emotional beings. He created us with the capacity to know, feel, and experience love. With the amazing gift of giving and receiving love comes the grueling work of grief when the object of our love departs. It's greatly encouraging to know and trust in the God who reigns victoriously over the heartache and pain that permeate this world. If we trust in the One who has overcome, then we ourselves are able to overcome. First John 5:5 assures us of this truth in saying, "Who is it that overcomes the world? Only the one who believes that Jesus is the Son of God." Do you believe?

pause to journal . . .

➤ Reflect upon God's healing power in the shadow of your loss. Consider the following questions and write your reflections in your Hope Journal.
  • What particular areas of healing are you in need of in the shadow of your loss?

- Have you allowed God to enter in and begin His healing work? If not, what barriers to healing can you identify?
- ๛ Reflect upon four Scriptures shared above pertaining to the promise of God's restorative work (Ps. 71:20–21; 1 Peter 5:10; John 16:33; 1 John 5:5). What stands out to you in these verses?

My Prayer for You, Fellow Mommy . . .

Dear Lord, fill my empty places. There are times when I feel so completely undone, Lord. I trust You to restore my life to all that You intend for it to be. I pray too, Lord, that You would bless this woman who reads here now and longs to experience Your restorative work in her own life. I pray that You would open her heart to receive You. I ask You, Lord, to do a miracle amidst the messiness of her grief. Give her eyes to see Your miraculous, healing, restorative action in her life. And Jesus, thank You for overcoming the world and reigning victoriously, so that we too may overcome the pains of this world. Amen.

Live It!

The beginning of this chapter describes the concept of emptiness as it relates to miscarriage and infant loss. Take inventory and identify which type(s) of emptiness (physical, emotional, or spiritual) you have struggled with the most or are currently struggling with. It may be one, two, or all three, and that's okay. Ask God in prayer to show you how you can fill that particular emptiness with more of Him. Additionally, read over the Hope for Today Bible verses throughout this chapter and ask yourself the following question: What evidence is there that I live as though I believe these truths? Apply these Scripture truths in your own life as you live in God's promise of restoration.

verses to live by —————————————————————

Then He who sat on the throne said, "Behold, I make all things new."

REVELATION 21:5 NKJV

৶ ৶

I have told you these things, so that in me you may have peace. In this world you will have trouble. But take heart! I have overcome the world.

JOHN 16:33

৶ ৶

Who is it that overcomes the world? Only the one who believes that Jesus is the Son of God.

1 JOHN 5:5

The Promise of Hope

Hope. We use that word so flippantly, don't we? Every day we go about
our lives, hoping for something. "I *hope* I can get all this laundry
done!" or "I *hope* the weather is nice today." Do either of those statements sound familiar? Sometimes our hopes are much more serious
than the mundane examples posed above. You may *hope* that your
husband gets that promotion at work so you can finally get caught up
on the bills. Maybe you have *hope* that today you have the strength
to get out of bed, shower, and do something productive, which may
not have been the case in the days following your loss. Or just maybe,
if you're like me, you have a *hope* to see your precious child again
someday. Whatever your hopes may be, however irrelevant or serious in the grand scheme of life, they mean something to you or you

wouldn't have them. Right? But how can we view hope from a biblical perspective? What does the Bible say about hope? Before we delve into answering such questions, let's take a moment to do a little exercise.

pause to journal . . .

&~ What "hopes" do you have today? Write them in your Hope Journal, however important or unimportant they may seem. Be honest!

We'll revisit this list as we proceed through this chapter. For now, let's delve into understanding what it means to possess a biblical hope; a hope beyond any kind of mere optimism or expectation. A hope that overflows. A hope in Christ. An eternal hope.

hope for today ——————————————————

We have this hope as an anchor for the soul, firm and secure.

HEBREWS 6:19

An Anchor for the Soul

At the beginning of the book we took a voyage through a ferocious storm. The storm was a parallel to my personal loss experiences. The life preserver that I spoke of was none other than my precious Jesus. In a similarly analogous fashion, a ship's anchor represents the biblical hope that I know and cling to. Elements of this hope, a promised hope from God, have been woven throughout every promise described in this book. We have learned . . .

Jesus is the ultimate promise, our promised hope!

God's *love* gives us hope for eternity.

God's *goodness* helps us realize He works all things for good.

God has a *purpose* and plan for our lives, despite our losses.

God is our one true source of *comfort*.

The *peace* of God pieces our broken hearts together.

In surrender, God *refines* our lives and hearts in the shadow of loss.

God takes our emptiness and *restores* us, making us strong, firm, and steadfast.

Hope flows through each of God's promises as described above. Romans 5:5 assures us that "hope does not put us to shame, because God's love has been poured out into our hearts through the Holy Spirit, who has been given to us." God's hope doesn't leave us frustrated, disappointed, or disillusioned because it's a promise that will never be broken. As we liken hope to an *anchor for the soul*, we must consider the purpose of a ship's anchor—to keep the ship from drifting due to winds or storms. Think back to the stormy voyage that we embarked upon in the introduction of this book and place yourself back in that boat. A storm rushes in, threatening to steer you off course, yet this time, an anchor keeps your location firm and secure. When we visualize our hope as an anchor for the soul, we see that this promised hope keeps our hearts and souls in tune with Jesus, who is our hope. Thus, when the storm of loss threatens our faith, our hope—our anchor for the soul—keeps us firm and secure in our faith.

The following passage of Scripture from *The Message* gives us a visual picture of what it looks like to possess this biblical hope that we've learned about:

> We who have run for our very lives to God have every reason to grab the promised hope with both hands and never let go. It's an unbreakable spiritual lifeline, reaching past all appearances right to the very presence of God where Jesus, running on ahead of us, has taken up his permanent post as high priest for us, in the order of Melchizedek. (Heb. 6:18–20)

This passage describes hope as a "promised hope." Promised. That's right . . . God's hope is a "promise"! When you think of the word *promise*, what comes to mind? According to the *Merriam-Webster Dictionary*, the word *promise* means "a declaration that one will do or refrain from doing something specified." A secondary definition asserts that a promise gives "reason to expect something." When we look at these definitions and insert God's promise of hope into the equation, it makes perfect sense to see that God is the one who is making the declaration to "do or refrain from doing something specified." It is He who gives us a "reason to expect something." In Hebrews 6:17–18 from *The Message*, we learn more about God's promises:

> When God wanted to guarantee his promises, he gave his word, a rock-solid guarantee—God can't break his word. And because his word cannot change, the promise is likewise unchangeable.

With God, there are no broken promises. His promises are guaranteed. His Word never changes and, therefore, neither do His promises. So what does it mean to have a "promised hope" from God, as stated in Hebrews 6:17–18 above? Simply stated, if God says He is going to do something, He will do it. When God's Word says that we ought to grab on to this promised hope with both hands, I think we should! After all, He says it's an unbreakable spiritual lifeline that takes us to God Himself, through Jesus.

pause to journal . . .

- What metaphor is used to describe this "promised hope"? What does that mean to you?
- Reflect upon your own pursuit of this promised hope. What needs to change for you to be the kind of person who is running for your very life to grab on to this promised hope in Christ?

hope for today ————————————————

Let us hold unswervingly to the hope we profess, for he who promised is faithful.

HEBREWS 10:23

A Living, Eternal Hope

As mommies with hope, the hope we profess is a living hope, described as such because our hope is focused on Christ, who lives. Such a hope did not appear in an instant as I faced my losses. It took time, prayer, and God's work in my life for me to understand. Below is a post from the blog, detailing some of what God has taught me about a living, eternal hope in Christ.

I have to admit, when I entered that ultrasound [when pregnant with Chloe] I hoped to go home with some good pictures. I hoped to get to record a video. I hoped to find out the sex. I hoped many, many things. Then, all of my hopes came crashing down when I heard the harsh words of my doctor: "Your baby is going to die." All I could feel in that moment were the hopes and dreams I had for my baby unraveling right before my eyes.

Hope. It took on an entirely new definition. Hope. It was my pregnancy with her, anticipating her death, that drove me to my knees. Hope. Found in the promises of His Word. Hope. Discovered as I wept and wailed at His feet. Hope. Revealed so boldly when her daddy gave his heart to Jesus in the aftermath of her death. Hope. In the big brown eyes of her brother who proudly declares her heavenly dwelling. Hope. In the innocence of a baby sister who never knew her, yet clings to Chloe's blankie as if she knows it's something special.

Hope. A confidence in knowing what lies ahead. Hope. Trusting in God's grace, which ushered my precious Chloe into heaven.

Hope. A promise to be fulfilled for those who are in Christ. Hope. For that unimaginable reunion. Hope. To press on, trudging through the deepest, darkest valley, to then climb to the top of the mountain where God's glory is revealed. Hope. In the miracle of His creation of this tiny baby girl. Hope. God used her life to transform me into a mommy with hope.

The one true source of my hope eternal . . . Jesus. *Where is your hope?*

hope for today

Praise be to the God and Father of our Lord Jesus Christ! In his great mercy he has given us new birth into a living hope through the resurrection of Jesus Christ from the dead, and into an inheritance that can never perish, spoil or fade. This inheritance is kept in heaven for you, who through faith are shielded by God's power until the coming of the salvation that is ready to be revealed in the last time.

1 PETER 1:3–5

Trusting in a living hope, made possible only by Jesus Christ's resurrection from the dead, secures for us eternity in heaven. Is that not the greatest hope you can imagine?

pause to journal . . .

&> Read the following verses from Scripture:
- Psalm 62:5–6
- Lamentations 3:24–26
- Romans 8:23–25

&> For each, share what God's Word has to say about hope and record it in your Hope Journal.

hope for today ————————————————————————

You do not grieve like the rest of mankind, who have no hope.

1 THESSALONIANS 4:13

Grieving with Hope

First Thessalonians 4:13–14 provides us with a great lesson on biblical hope. These verses encourage us by saying,

> Brothers and sisters, we do not want you to be uninformed about those who sleep in death, so that you do not grieve like the rest of mankind, who have no hope. For we believe that Jesus died and rose again, and so we believe that God will bring with Jesus those who have fallen asleep in him.

Let me first explain that in the Bible, the word *sleep* is referring to the state of those who have died and entered into heaven. Paul is explaining that, unlike the rest of mankind, believers in Jesus grieve *with* hope. Because Jesus overcame the grave through His miraculous resurrection from the dead, we have hope that when Jesus returns, He will bring with Him all those who have died. They will "wake up"; they will live again. As believers, we can grieve with hope. Even in the midst of our grief, we can live with hope—for our babies and for ourselves—because of the wonderful truth that Christ is alive!

pause to journal . . .

- What does it look like to grieve with hope?
- Are you grieving with hope?

My Prayer for You, Fellow Mommy . . .
Dearest Father, thank You for Your promises. What's more, thank You for being true to Your promises. Lord, I pray that You would replace any feelings of hopelessness with a hope in You. For the woman reading this book, God, I pray that You would reveal to her the hope that is found in Your Son, Jesus. Impress it upon her heart, Father, to look to Jesus as her one true source of hope for eternity in heaven. Thank You for this promise of hope, Oh Lord. In Jesus' precious name I pray. Amen.

Live It!
Revisit the list of "hopes" that you recorded in your Hope Journal at the beginning of this chapter and take some time to reflect on those items. How would you say your list of hopes lines up with what you have learned about in Scripture on the topic of hope? Which of them truly matter in light of eternity? If you feel so led, create a new list of hopes to tuck away in your Bible and refer to this list during devotion time or whenever you may be feeling the need for a reminder of God's promised hope in Christ.

verses to live by ────────────────

Let us hold unswervingly to the hope we profess, for he who promised is faithful.

HEBREWS 10:23

Ẃ Ẃ

May the God of hope fill you with all joy and peace as you trust in him, so that you may overflow with hope by the power of the Holy Spirit.

ROMANS 15:13

Ẃ Ẃ

We have this hope as an anchor for the soul, firm and secure.

HEBREWS 6:19

10

The Promise of Eternity

hope for today

How lovely is your dwelling place, LORD Almighty!

PSALM 84:1

In the middle of a city forty-five miles from my house, lies a cemetery. It's like most any other large cemetery you might imagine, hilly and green with trees spaced meticulously throughout the landscape, offering the perfect amount of shade for loved ones visiting those who have gone before. As you turn into the park-like setting, the hot asphalt curves around a pond, seemingly sunken into the earth. Ducks and geese waddle between the road and the water's edge. Some float in the still waters while others flock toward a toddling child who pinches off pieces of bread with glee and awkwardly tosses them to the ground. The paved road winds farther back without an end in sight. One can loop and turn and go in circles for what seems like miles. Yet, our hearts set to autopilot as we cross the gates of that place where the dead rest. The navigation of our souls knows just where to go as we cruise around every curve and bend that leads us to our destination: our daughter's grave.

Dwelling Place

We travel deep into the cemetery, beyond the graves of many. I often wonder, *What were these people like? How did they live their lives? With whom did they live their lives? Were they young or old?* Then, in a quaint section toward the back of the cemetery lies an area surrounded by the precious blooms of miniature lilac trees, so very fitting for the tiny graves within, encompassed by their beauty. We park along the road and follow a newly paved red cement path that is about as wide as my three-year-old is tall. We walk the path, facing a fully grown oak tree that has served many a purpose—cool shade on those hot Iowa summer days as tears poured just as easily as the sweat that beaded on the surface of my skin; the umbrella for family picnics after church on Sunday afternoons; home base for a game of tag; a refuge as we gaze upon her big brother running and chasing bubbles, bubbles she would have loved, while we sit in peaceful remembrance. All the while, making memories. Bittersweet.

The pathway divides this area of the land into two sides, and as we proceed to the end of the walkway, the path gives way to grass. Several steps farther, tiptoeing on the edge of ground that has been unearthed and awaits new growth of grass overtop graves, we see her stone. A rose-colored granite, polished to perfection on front and back, outlined with a rough-textured edge. A beautiful setting; a beautiful stone. Both for a beautiful girl. Yet this is not her home. She does not dwell here. She dwells in the house of the Lord, and oh how lovely it must be! "How lovely is your dwelling place, Lord Almighty" (Ps. 84:1), adorns the backside of Chloe's headstone for a reason. Let me explain.

We were as prepared as we could be on the day of Chloe's birth (and death). We had her blankie, her tiny clothes, and a birth plan in order. Though contractions came upon us suddenly in the night, too soon, we were prepared. I'm thankful that we were ready from a logistical standpoint, but emotionally, I was inept. As a part of our preparation for that day, we had created a music CD for playing in the hospital room. I love music; it brings me such comfort. The music played all day long and truly came to serve as background noise to all the emotion that welled up deep within my soul. Chloe was born, living and breathing with ten tiny fingers and the most perfect little toes. Her full head of black hair made me smile as I gazed upon her tender curls. We knew right away that she wouldn't be with us long. Cherishing the moments we did have, our arms embraced her and my fingers stroked her cheeks as tears poured down my own.

I knew that she was fading—too fast. I asked my nurse Ann, "Will you check her?" Within moments, she gently placed the stethoscope on Chloe's chest and softly said, "I'm sorry . . . she's gone." The next words she spoke struck me as I heard her say: "Time of death 3:55 p.m." As she verbalized one of the most difficult statements I've ever heard in my life, the background music that had been playing all along overwhelmed me with lyrics that provided a comfort that surpassed any earthly understanding. Amidst the wails and cries of my heart, a familiar tune continued to play. Based on Psalm 84, the song begins, "How lovely is your dwelling place, O Lord Almighty." The chorus proclaims, "Better is one day in your courts than thousands elsewhere." In the deepest pain of that moment, a moment when I felt dead inside, God brought the greatest comfort to my soul as He assured me that Chloe was with Him. In His dwelling place. Ann was right; *she was gone.* Gone from my world, but dwelling in the courts of my Lord!

hope for today ————————————————————

Better is one day in your courts than a thousand elsewhere.

PSALM 84:10

I can't claim to know what heaven is like, but I can imagine its glory. Scripture gives us a glimpse of heaven's glory. Let's dig in to God's Word and learn more about His dwelling place.

pause to journal . . .

ॐ Read the following passages of Scripture:
- Revelation 21:19–21
- John 14:1–6
- Psalm 84:4
- Revelation 21:4
- Hebrews 4:14
- Mark 16:19

ॐ For each of the passages above, share what God's Word has to say about heaven in your Hope Journal.

ॐ Did you learn anything new from these verses? What comfort do these verses bring as you contemplate your baby's eternal dwelling?

hope for today ———————————————

I write these things to you who believe in the name of the Son of God so that you may know that you have eternal life.

1 JOHN 5:13

That You May Know

I realize that some of you may be wrestling with whether your baby is in heaven. This is a very real question that you may have pondered since your loss. Some of you may look at such a question and boldly proclaim with confidence, "Yes, she's there!" while others of you may not be so sure. There are several verses in Scripture that provide great comfort and evidence for the truth that our babies are with God in

His dwelling place. God gives us His Word so that we may know the truth about such matters and have hope. In fact, Psalm 119 uses the phrase, "I have put my hope in your word" four times (vv. 74. 81, 114, 147), as the psalmist expresses his gratitude for and understanding of God's Word. The gospel of John begins by noting the significance of the Word by saying, "In the beginning was the Word, and the Word was with God, and the Word was God. He was with God in the beginning" (John 1:1–2). Verse 14 of that same passage goes on to say, "The Word became flesh and made his dwelling among us. We have seen his glory, the glory of the one and only Son, who came from the Father, full of grace and truth." Jesus is the Word. The Word is truth. We can know, trust, and believe in the Word!

So what does Jesus say about children? The very fact that Jesus came into the world as a baby Himself speaks volumes to me. In the shadow of loss, you've likely experienced a sense of devaluation of your baby's life; as if his or her tiny life did not matter. Sadly, others may fail to acknowledge the significance of these babies' lives. Yet to think that God Almighty sent His own Son into this world as a helpless baby brings me solace. Such truth demonstrates to me that God Himself sees value in the life of a baby.

As Jesus grew into a man and was active in ministry, He also demonstrated a deep love and appreciation for children. When the disciples rebuked the children for approaching Jesus as He was teaching, Jesus stopped them and said, "Let the little children come to me, and do not hinder them, for the kingdom of heaven belongs to such as these" (Matt. 19:14). When the disciples asked Jesus who was the greatest in the kingdom of heaven, He replied by saying, "Truly I tell you, unless you change and become like little children, you will never enter the kingdom of heaven. Therefore, whoever takes the lowly position of this child is the greatest in the kingdom of heaven" (18:3–4). Also in the gospel of Matthew, Jesus is found defending the children in the temple who were praising Him, recognizing that He truly is the Messiah. The children witnessed Jesus' miraculous healing and shouted out, "Hosanna to the Son of David" (21:15). When others questioned the children's praise, Jesus quoted Scripture from the Old Testament in saying, "From the lips of children and infants you, Lord, have called forth your praise" (v. 16; see also Ps. 8:2). We should also consider the story of David from the Old Testament. His son died as an infant at seven days old. Stricken with grief, he still had hope as he declared, "I will go to him, but he will not return to me" (2 Sam. 12:23). David, known as a man after God's own heart, was a sinner like the rest of us. His faith and trust in a merciful God, however, declared him righteous. It is his faith that enabled him to have a confident hope and expectation to be reunited with his son in heaven.

When we received Chloe's diagnosis and faced her imminent death, I had no doubts about *her* eternal dwelling. I trusted that God's love and mercy welcomed her into heaven at the very moment she took her last breath. During my pregnancy with her and shortly after her death, I realized for the first time that I could know with certainty where *I* was headed upon my earthly death. I imagined what it would be like to see her again in heaven. Questions surfaced, some of which linger still. Questions like, Will she know me? What will she look like? Will she be a tiny baby or a big girl? How will I find her there? How do I know I am going there? Perhaps you have asked similar questions in the shadow of your own loss experience, and quite possibly there are questions that remain.

I admit that I don't have all the answers. I do, however, know the One who does and that is enough. My Jesus is enough. He tells me He's enough (2 Cor. 12:9). By definition, faith is "confidence in what we hope for and assurance about what we do not see" (Heb. 11:1). I'm sure of this promised hope from God. In 1 John 5:13, God's Word boldly proclaims, "I write these things to you who believe in the name of the Son of God so that you may know that you have eternal life." So that you may know. We aren't guaranteed a sneak peek at how God will choose to weave together the story of our lives on earth. We do not have the privilege of seeing the big picture from beginning to end.

However, if we know and believe in His Son, we are assured of the end result—eternity in heaven, His dwelling place.

pause to journal . . .

ৈ Write down the questions you have about heaven in your Hope Journal now.

ৈ In prayer, ask God to bring you peace, wisdom, and understanding as you seek the truth about your questions through His Word.

hope for today

He has made everything beautiful in its time. He has also set eternity in the human heart; yet no one can fathom what God has done from beginning to end.

ECCLESIASTES 3:11

Impacted for Eternity

Forever changed. Two simple words that validate, acknowledge, and give meaning. What if we allowed this change that we've experienced to impact our lives for eternity? What if we let God turn the hurt and the pain into something worth remembering, something with eternal ramifications?

My husband wrote the following for the *Mommies with Hope* blog as he contemplated the significance of Chloe's impact on his own life, a life that is changed, now and forevermore.

Hearing the kids play, laugh, and say funny things puts a father's mind at ease, telling him that he's been doing a good job and he can enjoy it. Then you hear a song that puts your heart and mind back to a past that is hard to deal with and you sometimes just lose it in a moment. Hearing Stephen Curtis Chapman's "Cinderella" and remembering Chloe in that moment took me back to when I was holding her in my arms, but it wasn't joyful at the time, it was sorrowful.

After four years I still have a very hard time talking about it, but one thing I don't have a problem with talking about is the one thing that I will forever thank her and my Savior for, my salvation and humbling toward God. Chloe brought me closer to God than anyone before. It didn't happen overnight. But, after some crying, anger, sadness, and depression, I heard the Lord's message through the church we started going to, Lakeside Fellowship. I remember I started having hope again and I was asked if I wanted to do a Bible study with the pastor and another guy that I have grown a great friendship with.

We started reading through the book of John and I remembered reading some of this stuff in my early college days. I started reading the Bible more and more and the picture of Jesus started making more sense than it had in years. I remember the first sermon at the church we started going to and I learned more in an hour than I had the previous four years.

After a few weeks, on September 11, 2006, I accepted God's gift of grace and redemption into his kingdom. While me, my wife, and another friend prayed while I was accepting this gift, I remember a burden being lifted off my shoulders. It was like I didn't have to worry about Chloe anymore, because I knew she was being taken care of in heaven with my Lord and Savior. This does not mean I don't grieve. I think about her every day, at least once if not more . . . but I don't worry for her, I long to see her again. I know when I do pass on from this life and go to heaven, I will dance with her every chance I get. As the song played in my head I imagined myself dancing with her, knowing that the clock will never strike midnight when I see her again!

It is my deepest desire that you too are forever changed, impacted for eternity with a hope in Christ that prevails over any earthly trial. For now, we keep moving—one foot in front of the other. There are tough days and tears will fall. Yet, may the One who holds each tear also be the keeper of your heart as you place your hope in Him. May your hope be eternal as you live in God's ultimate promise—the hope of His Son, Jesus. May you become a mommy with hope, living each day in the abundant promises God has in store for you.

verses to live by ————————————————

Blessed are those who dwell in your house; they are ever praising you.

PSALM 84:4

LORD Almighty, blessed is the one who trusts in you.

PSALM 84:12

My Prayer for You, Fellow Mommy . . .

Dearest Eternal Father in Heaven, thank You for giving me hope in Your promise of eternity. Through Your Son, Jesus, You bestow hope for today, hope for tomorrow, and hope everlasting. This is Your promise, and Lord, I am thankful! I pray, Lord, that this woman would come to a place where she too would cling to these truths. May she know the promise of Your love and rest in the hope of eternity for her and for her precious baby who is with You now. Lead her to a place of trusting in the very great and precious promises that You have in store for her. Lord, I know that the woman who trusts in You shall also dwell with You in eternity. Thank You for this promise! Amen.

Appendix A

Becoming a Mommy with Hope

A mommy with hope possesses the eternal hope of heaven found in Jesus Christ. A mommy with hope . . .

Acknowledges that she is a sinner, like everyone else . . .

"For all have sinned and fall short of the glory of God." Romans 3:23

Knows that there is a price for her sin . . .

"For the wages of sin is death." Romans 6:23

Believes that Jesus Christ died to pay for her sin . . .

"But God demonstrates his own love for us in this: While we were still sinners, Christ died for us." Romans 5:8

Understands that God wants to save her from her sin . . .

"If you declare with your mouth, 'Jesus is Lord,' and believe in your heart that God raised him from the dead, you will be saved." Romans 10:9

Has received eternal life in heaven . . .

"Everyone who calls on the name of the Lord will be saved."
Romans 10:13

A Prayer of Hope . . .

Dearest heavenly Father, thank You for being the God who loves me, in spite of my sin. I admit that I am a sinner, Lord. I realize that You have made a way for me through Your Son, Jesus Christ. I pray that You would forgive me of my sin. I ask You, Lord Jesus, to come into my heart so that I may live solely for You. Thank You for living a perfect life, dying an undeserved death on the cross for me, for paying the penalty that I deserved, and for overcoming the cross through Your resurrection from the dead. I trust in You, Jesus, the giver of a pure and true eternal hope. Amen.

One day, the mommy with hope will undoubtedly experience a sweet and longed-for reunion in heaven, and oh what a day that will be!

If you have entered into a saving relationship with the Lord Jesus Christ and now possess an eternal hope in Him, I would love to rejoice with you, my fellow mommy! Please tell me about it by emailing me at: teske@mommieswithhope.com.

Appendix B

Fellow Mommies' "Hope Stories"

Throughout the book, excerpts of various women's "hope stories" have been woven in as they relate to the topic under study. Below, you'll find five women's stories in their own words. I pray that these Hope Stories bring you comfort.

Jill

In August 2008 we experienced a miscarriage—pain and loss you never understand until you're in the midst of it yourself. I only knew I was pregnant for fifteen days—doesn't seem long, but once you've connected with a child, it is a bond you share for life. I never felt the baby move, saw her face or heard her voice, but yet the baby is mine.

The days following the loss were difficult; tears would come from things I never expected. I'd see a baby toy and wonder if we'd ever need that again, I'd look at the kids' pictures on the wall and realize I wouldn't need to rearrange them nine months down the road, and once my three-year-old asked me to read the book, "We've Lost our Baby." She didn't understand why it made me cry.

During the time of sadness there was also strength; not mine, but God's. He lifted me up in ways I hadn't experienced. The loss was real, but His comfort was too. Even when I wasn't seeking Him, He was holding me. When the hurt created questions and caused me to push away, He drew me close.

Looking back it's still hard to understand, and thinking about our little one still brings tears. But God's Word is true; He has a plan and it's one for good. I would never say losing a child is good, but what God did through the experience has been. He made Himself real and proved His Word to be true. He worked through others and lifted me up. He reminded me, we have hope and heaven is real.

And nearly six months following, He unexpectedly blessed me with another pregnancy. Early on there was fear. What if I lost this baby too? I didn't want to walk that road again. As our pregnancy reached the six-week mark, thoughts turned to the baby we should have delivered in six weeks and feelings of joy turned to ones of guilt. I rejoiced for the baby to come, but felt like I was forgetting the one who already was.

Time went on and God continued to walk me through this journey we call life. I would cry; He'd dry the tears. I would question; He would answer. He assured me my pain was OK, the loss was real, and He knew; He'd lost a child too.

So as the pregnancy progressed I found myself thinking about names. Even with all the suggestions, I always came back to Jenae. I'm not sure why, but it seemed to be the name God had for our little one. Eventually I looked into its meaning and found it to be, "God has given." Since this wasn't a baby we had "planned," I thought the name fit.

Then it was time to move on to the middle name; instantly Jenae Hope entered my world. It made sense—God has given hope, and what a gift that is!!

Without even knowing the sex of our baby I was sure we had a little Jenae Hope Beran.

That confidence only lasted to the halfway point of our pregnancy. We had always waited for the doctor to announce the baby's sex in the delivery room, but this time my curiosity surprised me.

At the completion of our ultrasound, the radiologist handed me an envelope with the answer to my question. I waited awhile, but eventually peaked and pledged to a twenty-week secret—it was a boy!

I wasn't totally surprised as there had been similarities in this pregnancy with that of our other son, but because of the name it seemed God had given, I was prepared for a girl. I can remember thinking, "What about Jenae?"

And though I didn't hear God's voice, it was as if He said, "I'm already holding her." And then there was peace—it all made sense—that name was on my heart during the time she should have been born. I thought I was naming baby number five, but God knew it was number four.

The name doesn't make it any easier; actually it brings the tears right back. But I'm learning that's OK, though her life was short, her presence was real and the pain is too. She's one I won't hold until heaven, but I'm thankful for her life. I'm also grateful God has given us His hope! Mommy loves you little Jenae Hope Beran.

Lindsey

It was December 6, 2006, and I went to a routine doctor appointment and found out that I had lost my baby around eighteen weeks. I was told by my doctor that I had to deliver at the hospital. On December 7 we went to Methodist Hospital and checked in. By God's sovereignty, our nurse was a longtime friend from church. I was in labor for about seven hours until I finally gave birth to a baby boy around 5:30 in the evening. We decided to name him Will since it was God's will that he not be born, but live forever in heaven with Jesus. That day I was so strong and didn't shed a single tear even when I was holding him in my arms. That was only by God's power that I could be that strong. The next day was hard. I was leaving the maternity ward with no baby. I remember the next couple of weeks being very emotional and only wanting to be with my family and God. I prayed a lot but never got mad at God. I knew he had a plan for my life, and it was better than anything I could ever imagine. My body went through the same things that it went through after having my first two babies. My milk came in and I remember that being a constant reminder of what I just went through. Overall, I was very tough and strong because, after all, I am a believer and this was God's plan. Being tough and strong isn't always a good thing. I was holding in my grief and not letting people see that you can believe in Jesus but still be sad. I was more worried about what everyone else would think.

In March of the following year I went on a weekend retreat in the wilderness. It was all about spending time with the Lord. The Lord completely broke me on this retreat. I have never cried so much in my life. Everything that we were learning and applying brought all my grief to the surface. I know God used that weekend to show me that I don't have to be strong on my own. He is there when I am sad and He will help me through whatever comes my way. God loves me and doesn't want to see me in pain. He holds every tear in His hand and whether I know it or not, He is right there beside me. A portion of Scripture that comforts me is Psalm 139:15–16: "You watched me as I was being formed in utter seclusion, as I was woven together in the dark of the womb. You saw me before I was born. Every day of my life was recorded in your book. Every moment was laid out before a single day had passed" (NLT). This Scripture gives me the hope that one day I will be reunited with Will in heaven!

Rachel

It was September 11. On the radio, they were talking about 9/11, the day of the terrorist attacks on the United States. As I listened, I had the feeling I would soon be facing my own kind of disaster.

I was eleven weeks pregnant with our second child. I had been spotting lightly for several days. Since no other symptoms of miscarriage accompanied it, and I had read online that some spotting in early pregnancy was perfectly normal, I decided not to get overly concerned. This day the spotting was heavier. I decided to see a doctor.

The doctor was reassuring. Even after checking me, he said it was probably nothing to be concerned about. Still, to put my mind at ease, he said he would do an "in-house" ultrasound. Hearing the baby's heartbeat would make me feel better.

I felt nervous as I laid down on that cold table in the ultrasound room. The doctor started moving the monitor over my jelly-covered belly. I waited for the sweet sound of a heartbeat. I kept waiting.

I searched the doctor's face for some kind of answer. He was trying not to show emotion, but I could sense his panic. He wasn't expecting this. He continued to search. My own heart was speeding in my chest. Tears welled up in my eyes.

Finally, he quit searching. He quickly apologized and reassured me that it was probably just his error. I asked if this had ever happened before. He hesitantly, yet honestly answered, "No." I knew the truth.

While the clinic scheduled a hospital ultrasound, I called my husband and broke down. We really wanted this baby. We had been making plans and choosing names. How could this be happening? Alan offered reassuring words and promised to get there quickly.

The hospital ultrasound was quite clear. No movement. No heartbeat. Our baby had only developed to six weeks.

We were sent home to wait. Tears flowed from our broken hearts. I went about my normal activities trying to forget what I was waiting for. I was still spotting, yet experiencing heightened pregnancy symptoms. It was emotionally and physically depleting.

I had two more ultrasounds, then to avoid an infection, I had a D&C on September 25. That was a hard day.

Although many offered reassuring words, I found that, as I grieved, the most comforting and reassuring words were those in the Bible, God's holy Word.

God's Word tells us that we can trust Him, even when we don't understand (Prov. 3:5). He helps us in our distress (Rom. 8:26). He holds us securely in His hand (John 10:28). He comforts us in all our troubles (2 Cor. 1:4). He causes everything to work together for our good (Rom. 8:28).

As I chose to cling to God and His Word, it still wasn't easy, but I felt His love surround me. I found hope for the future and peace that truly passed all comprehension. Words can't adequately describe it, but He comforted my heart in ways only He could.

What a joy to know that we never have to process life alone. He cares. He helps. He comforts. He holds us securely. We can trust Him, even when we don't understand and wonder why.

Through the birth of our second healthy baby and a second pregnancy loss, I can say God is faithful and His Word holds true. I know that when I choose to trust Him, I can have peace and hope through all of life's circumstances, both joyful and sorrowful.

I praise God for the two healthy children that I get to hold here on earth, realizing we should never take the miracle of life for granted.

I also praise Him for the two children He holds for us in Heaven and I look forward to meeting them someday.

Although it sounds strange, through our losses, I have gained much. My faith has been strengthened. I know true hope and peace. I can comfort others, the way I have been comforted. Even in having the opportunity to share this with you, I am reminded that there is purpose in the pain. Only God could take such heartache and use it for good.

Of all the words I've shared with you, I believe the most reassuring words are those from God's Word. Cling to Him and His Word. I can truly say, if you choose to trust Him, He will comfort and strengthen you as only He can.

RaeLynn

When my husband and I found out that I was pregnant with our first child, we were excited to begin this next chapter of our lives. My first trimester began very smoothly, and we assumed that things were going well. At our first ultrasound appointment, our obstetrician indicated that the baby's bladder looked a bit enlarged, but that it was "probably nothing." I didn't want my worrisome nature to overshadow the joy of my pregnancy, so I forced myself to dismiss it as well. Nothing could have prepared me for what was to come.

At our eighteen-week appointment, as soon as I saw the large black spot on the ultrasound screen, I knew something was terribly wrong. The technician wordlessly completed the ultrasound and then left the room for what seemed like hours. When the doctor returned, he informed us that the ultrasound indicated some abnormalities and that he wanted to refer us to a perinatologist for further consultation. He explained that the large black spot was our baby's enlarged bladder, but he was also concerned about some findings on the ultrasound which were indicative of Down's syndrome.

The next day, after a more thorough ultrasound and an amniocentesis, the perinatologist we had been referred to sat us down and delivered a shocking diagnosis. Our baby had an enlarged bladder due to a blockage, abnormal kidneys, cystic hygromas, and a heart defect. She said that our baby's condition was "incompatible with life." She explained that we would have to make the decision about whether or not to continue the pregnancy. I sobbed as I had never before in my life as my world came out from beneath me.

That weekend was Mother's Day. We traveled back to our hometown to be with our family. I cried the entire trip as I read the booklet that the doctor had given us. Something that I remember reading was that God's heart was breaking as well, and He was grieving with us. That gave me great comfort as I tried to process the news that had been given to us. As we told our families that weekend, we were met with many tears but were told again and again that they would support us no matter what we decided. Ultimately, we decided to continue the pregnancy as long as my health was not at risk.

Not wanting to give up, I underwent numerous tests and procedures the next few weeks and consulted with two different perinatologists. A kidney analysis was done to assess our baby's kidney function. Sadly, the results indicated that his kidneys were not functioning normally, which meant that he was not a candidate for any further intervention.

I had no amniotic fluid, which was critical to lung development. He would be born with virtually no lung capacity and would not survive.

At that point, we had a definite shift in our thinking. While we had spent so many weeks tirelessly seeking out ways to save our baby's life, we had lost sight of the fact that our time with him was fleeting. During the final months of my pregnancy, we spent many hours watching our son on ultrasound during our prenatal appointments. Our favorite tech would talk about how he was "as happy as a clam" as she showed us pictures of him yawning or squirming around in my tummy. We also played music and read stories to our son each night. We prayed to God to cherish the time that we did have with him, and even though it was extremely hard, we found the courage and the strength to go on. We planned to name him Dominic, which means "belonging to God."

I went into labor nine weeks early. His birth was so bittersweet—we were happy to finally meet Dominic, but sorrow was upon us because we knew he couldn't stay. Dominic was enveloped in love that day. We held him, dressed him, and gave him a bath. We took countless pictures and received treasured mementos, including a lock of his hair, his hospital bracelet, and a plaster mold of his hand. Dominic was with us for ninety minutes before he was called to his heavenly home. We find great comfort in knowing that Dominic felt only love in his short life. We long for the day when we will be with him again, but until then, we know that he is experiencing the joy that only comes from being with Jesus.

Theresa

A year ago, I was pregnant for the first time. Even though I had just turned thirty-nine, I felt like my life was just beginning. My first doctor appointment at ten weeks started with an ultrasound. I vividly recall the moment I saw my baby on the screen. I was completely overwhelmed with awe and love for my baby. Until then it had felt somewhat surreal, but there she was. Of course it was far too early to tell the baby's sex, but I knew this was the little girl I had always dreamed of. The technician didn't say anything, just took some measurements. When she was done, the technician calmly told me that it wasn't what she would expect for ten weeks and that she would need to have a doctor look at the printouts and measurements. She sent me back out to the waiting room to sit with all the pregnant ladies for half an hour while I tried to fight back the fears swirling through my mind. When I was finally called back in, the doctor told me that the fetus had stopped developing at eight weeks. At first I didn't understand what he was telling me. When I finally realized that my baby was gone, I was absolutely crushed. I spent the next several days crying my eyes out, praying for a miracle and hoping that somehow the doctor had made a mistake. I even made an appointment for another ultrasound at a different clinic to get a second opinion. But before the second ultrasound, I miscarried and there was no more denying it. In the days and weeks that followed I alternated between blaming God, blaming Satan, and blaming myself for my baby's death. But mostly I blamed myself. Night after night I dreamed that I was taking care of a baby and every time something horrible happened to the baby. Gradually, with the help of a Christian counselor, I worked through my feelings of grief and guilt, but I continued to struggle with whether or not God would ever allow me to be a mother here on earth.

Several months after the miscarriage, my pastor preached from the book of Jonah. When I read the second chapter of Jonah it really resonated with me, particularly verses 5 and 6:

> The engulfing waters threatened me,
>   the deep surrounded me;
>   seaweed was wrapped around my head.
> To the roots of the mountains I sank down;
>   the earth beneath barred me in forever.
> But you, Lord my God,
>   brought my life up from the pit.

The imagery of the waves washing over him, sinking down to the depth of the ocean with seaweed entangling him, I could certainly identify with those feelings. But what astounded me was that Jonah had such faith that from *inside the fish* he could say, "But you, LORD my God, brought my life up from the pit." My pastor talked about how the story of Jonah has a theme that recurs throughout the Bible. First a defeat, then a time of hiding, and then power and rescue. I thought about how that applied to me. First the loss of my baby, then the struggling with what the future might hold for me. I trusted that next would come the power and rescue.

Two weeks after what would have been my due date I took a home pregnancy test and, wonder of wonders, it was positive! God had heard me and had answered my prayers! It was the miracle I was hoping for! And then, just a week later, I started spotting and, in a few days, that baby was gone as well. It was as if the whale had spit me back out into the ocean. I was crushed again, drowning again, wondering what I had done to deserve this a second time.

So now here I am again, trying to be able to accept not having a child here on earth if that's what God's will for me is, but desperately wanting a child. I take comfort in knowing that I have two children waiting for me in Heaven. I thank God that even though in the eyes of the world they really didn't amount to anything, He loved them enough to die for them. Ultimately, that is where my hope is, where I know without a doubt the power and rescue is.

Appendix C

About Mommies with Hope

Mommies with Hope is a biblically based support group ministry for women who have experienced the loss of a child, born out of two women's personal experiences with loss. Together, Teske Drake and Lindsay Farmer stepped out in obedience to comfort others with the same comfort that they received from God (2 Cor. 1), and the group began meeting in the fall of 2007. Groups currently meet in the Midwest and God continues to bless the growth of this ministry as He raises women up to offer groups in their own communities. If you are interested in starting a Mommies with Hope group in your community, please email Teske at teske@mommieswithhope.com.

Please visit the Mommies with Hope website (www.mommieswithhope .com) for a list of resources that I pray you will find helpful in the shadow of your loss.

Acknowledgments

God provided a way for me to take the first steps in this journey through two amazingly gifted authors and speakers: Lysa Terkeurst and Cecil Murphey. Thank you, Lysa, for the opportunity to attend the Proverbs 31 Ministries She Speaks Conference through the blog contest you hosted in 2010. Thank you, Cec, for your generosity in providing scholarships for the contest winners. Each of your ministries has impacted my walk and my writing in ways immeasurable.

To my new friends at Kregel—Dennis, Steve, Dawn, Cat, Rachel, Leah—each of you has been amazing to work with on this project. It has truly been a labor of love. Thank you!

The calling to write this book was revealed years ago, yet came to fruition only after some encouragement from the dearest of friends who knew about the tugging on my heart. Jen Diers and Tara Dekkers, your support, friendship, and encouragement through the toughest years in my life mean so much. I treasure you both, my faithful prayer warriors, who always encouraged me to live my calling.

To my fellow mommies—I cherish you, and this book is for you. Thank you for allowing me to share in this journey with you, both in the darkest of days and in times of rejoicing. Always remember, your precious babies' lives are significant and have the power in their legacy to reach the lost for eternity. What a treasure. Special thanks to Amanda, Deanna, Jill, Kimberlee, Lindsey, Nicole, Rachel, RaeLynn, and Theresa—fellow mommies who shared portions of their Hope

Stories for this important project. I trust God will use your stories to minister.

To Shayla Hood, truly a once-in-a-lifetime friend. I treasure the journey we've shared.

To Lindsay Farmer, a fellow mommy with a vision and a heart that is sold out for Jesus—you are a blessing, to me and to so many others. Step back and take a look at the impact of Andrew Lindsay's brief, yet precious life, sweet sister!

Thank you Pastor Dave Heisterkamp for believing in this ministry and for generously giving your time, support, wisdom, and gospel-centered love for those who are hurting, myself included.

Mom, thank you for believing in me and for being my best friend. I treasure our morning talks and your loving encouragement. I hope I've made you proud. To my niece, Kaylee, who has changed my world—I love you too! To my two earthly blessings, Gabe and Aiyana, I love you more than you will ever know. It is an amazing privilege to be your mommy and I am blessed beyond words. To my husband, Justin—you are my greatest encourager and the best daddy I know. Your support and blessing is a treasured gift. I am grateful.

Jesus—giver of all hope and fulfillment of the Father's promise—may You forever be honored and glorified as I continue to live out the calling You have placed on my life. I am humbly honored that You would ever use the lives of my precious babies to share hope with the hurting. My hope is in You alone.

About the Author

Inspired by her own experience through the loss of her newborn daughter, Chloe, in 2006, Teske Drake cofounded Mommies with Hope, a biblically based support group ministry for women who have experienced the loss of a child through miscarriage, stillbirth, or infant loss, established in 2007, and currently serves as president. In 2009, Teske experienced the miscarriage of Jesse at six weeks gestation, and Riyah Mae at fourteen weeks gestation. Drawing from her personal experiences with miscarriage and infant loss, in addition to the similar experiences of the many women to whom she has ministered, Teske has a passion for sharing the hope of Jesus Christ in coping with grief.

Teske Drake has earned her PhD in Human Development and Family Studies from Iowa State University, where she focused her research primarily on women's experiences with miscarriage and infant loss, and most recently their support experiences after loss through the Mommies with Hope ministry. Her professional experience consists of teaching courses in child and family development at the university level and developmental psychology for a local community college. Teske currently serves as the director of Hamilton's Academy of Grief and Loss, where she works to provide grief-related information, education, resources, and support to grieving children, families, and the community in central Iowa and across the state.

Teske and her husband, Justin, reside in central Iowa, caring for their two living children, Gabriel and Aiyana, and niece, Kaylee, and serve the Lord with joy through their church, Lakeside Fellowship.

What women are saying about
Hope for Today, Promises for Tomorrow

"The grief we as parents experience when a child leaves this life before we do is a pain deeper than words can express. In the shadow of your loss, I encourage you to find hope in the Lord and in His Word. *Hope for Today, Promises for Tomorrow: Finding Light Beyond the Shadow of Miscarriage or Infant Loss* is a precious resource that can help you to experience God's hope!"—**Michelle Duggar**, mother of TLC's *19 Kids & Counting*

"With compassionate strength, Teske . . . addresses the deep, engulfing pain of miscarriage and infant loss, including the difficult and sometimes unanswerable questions that accompany such tragedy. But she doesn't leave her reader there; Teske shares the treasures that can be found when we allow Jesus to walk alongside us through our suffering.

"Teske gently encourages grieving mothers to shift perspective; as we turn our focus from finite death to the eternal promises of God, hope fills our lives, and God miraculously redeems our losses. . . .

"While written to grieving mothers, this book is also a terrific resource for fathers, grandparents, aunts and uncles, friends, co-workers, and others grieving the loss of a child and/or seeking wisdom in how to support a grieving parent."—**Cheryl Darnell**, executive director of SIDS America

"I've experienced deep loss and heartache so crippling, I couldn't open my mouth without breaking into tears. If you've been to this place because of a miscarriage or infant loss and are ready to process these hard emotions, this is the book for you. With the tender voice of experience and empathy, Teske will take you on a journey of healing and hope."—**Lysa TerKeurst**, *New York Times* best-selling author and president of Proverbs 31 Ministries

"*Hope for Today, Promises for Tomorrow* is a compassionate and practical reminder of the promises God gives us in the shadow of loss. Through "Hope Journal" exercises and "Live It" activity suggestions, Teske enables readers to apply these promises personally, transforming them from abstract concepts into real hope. Her own story, as well as those of other women who have walked this road, will inspire you to believe that healing is possible. I love Teske's heart for hurting women, and highly recommend this book. It will be a great resource for individual or group study."—**Becky Avella**, author of *And Then You Were Gone: Restoring a Broken Heart After Pregnancy Loss*

"Teske's book, *Hope for Today, Promises for Tomorrow*, is a gracious and compassionate look at dealing with the loss of a child. As a mom who has lost children herself, and who also has the privilege of walking through that journey with other women, I am thankful for this resource. It is biblically based, permeated with Scripture, and tender as well. Thank you, Teske, for reminding me afresh of God's promises and for helping me minister to hurting moms."—**Janet Aucoin**, Women's Ministries Director, Faith Church, Lafayette, IN